KT-364-352

Anregungen
Entwürfe
Tipps & Tricks

Ideas
Designs
Tips & Tricks

Andreas Knobl

Porzellanmalerei
Exotische Vögel

Porcelain Painting
Exotic Birds

Callwey

— *Abb. 6 Der Autor Andreas Knobl*
— *Ill. 6 The author Andreas Knobl*

— *Abb. 7 Flugstudie eines Kakadus,*
  fotografiert in Australien (vgl. S. 67 f.
— *Ill. 7 A flight study of a cockatoo,*
  photographed in Australia (see p. 67 f.)

© 2003 der deutsch-englischen Ausgabe
Verlag Georg D.W. Callwey GmbH & Co. KG,
Streitfeldstraße 35, 81673 München
© 2003 by Georg D. W. Callwey GmbH & Co.
KG, Munich

Das Werk einschließlich aller seiner Teile ist
urheberrechtlich geschützt. Jede Verwertung
außerhalb der engen Grenzen des Urheber-
rechtsgesetzes ist ohne Zustimmung des Ver-
lages unzulässig und strafbar. Das gilt ins-
besondere für Vervielfältigungen, Über-
setzungen, Mikroverfilmungen und die Ein-
speicherung und Verarbeitung in elektro-
nischen Systemen.
All rights reserved. No part of this book may be
reprinted, translated, filmed or electroni-
cally transmitted.
www.callwey.de
E-mail: buch@callwey.de

Übersetzung ins Englische von
Janice Luther, Aumühle
Alle Fotos und Zeichnungen stammen vom
Autor bis auf: Abbildungen S. 16, 17, 91, 94
(Fotos von Lora, einem roten Ara): Sabine
Gossenbacher, CH-Münchenstein
Den Autor fotografierte Bettina Krinner,
Lenggries

Die Deutsche Bibliothek verzeichnet diese
Publikation in der Deutschen
Nationalbibliografie; detaillierte
bibliografische Daten sind im Internet über
<http://dnb.ddb.de> abrufbar.
Die Deutsche Bibliothek lists this publication in
the Deutsche Nationalbibliografie; detailed
bibliographic data is available in the
Internet at <http://dnb.ddb.de>.

ISBN 3-7667-1573-9

Reihengestaltung Johannes Steil, München
Umschlaggestaltung Callwey Verlag,
Andreas Funk, Alexander Stix, München
Satz Callwey Verlag, Andreas Funk,
München
Litho Callwey Verlag, Erasmus Winter,
München
Druck und Bindung Druckerei Appl,
Wemding

Printed in Germany 2003

Inhalt

Contents

Introduction

In my new book I am going to whisk you away into the colourful and fascinating world of parrots and other exotic birds.

Motifs of such birds offer inexhaustible possibilities for artistic interpretation, and are certainly one of the most attractive subjects for painting on porcelain.

This book will help you to overcome any anxieties you may have when you see these paintings for the first time and believe them to be difficult. It certainly is demanding work, but with the help of my fully comprehensible instructions (which I will give you step-by-step) I am trying to make it simpler for you. For an easy comprehension I have painted my step-by-step-work on porcelain and then photographed each step for you.

I have emphasized how important it is to have the basic technical know-how, and when you follow these tips and always bear them in mind every time you carry out your work, you will feel more confident and be more aware of what you are doing with your brush.

The requirements for high quality and efficiency are given to you every time. One does not exclude the other, but rather they go parallel to each other. The technical descriptions in this book do not only apply to painting birds, but can be used to master all sorts of other subjects, such as all kinds of animal and floral paint-

Einleitung

Mit meinem neuen Buch entführe ich Sie in die farbenprächtige und faszinierende Welt der Papageien und anderer exotischer Vögel.

Solche Vogelmotive bieten unerschöpfliche Möglichkeiten der malerischen Umsetzung und gehören wohl mit zu den attraktivsten Sujets, die man auf Porzellan malen kann.

Dieses Buch wird Ihnen helfen, bei dieser zunächst schwierig anmutenden Malerei Berührungsängste abzubauen. Es ist eine anspruchsvolle, aber doch mit genauer Anleitung nachvollziehbare Malerei, die ich Ihnen in vielen Schritt-für-Schritt-Darstellungen näher bringen möchte. Diese habe ich für Sie zum besseren Verständnis alle auf Porzellan gemalt und fotografiert. Wenn Sie die grundsätzlichen technischen Hinweise zum Know-how beachten, auf die ich in diesem Buch besonderen Wert gelegt habe, und sich diese immer wieder ins Gedächtnis rufen, werden Sie sich sicherer fühlen, und Ihnen wird jeden Moment während der Ausführung bewusst sein, was Sie mit Ihrem Pinsel gerade arbeiten.

So sind die Voraussetzungen für hohe Qualität und gleichzeitige Effizienz jederzeit gegeben. Denn beides schließt sich nicht aus, sondern geht parallel einher. Mit der in diesem Buch beschriebenen Technik sind Sie dann zudem nicht nur auf das Malen von Vögeln beschränkt, sondern beherrschen alle Arten von Tier- und Blumenmalereien in dieser Manier. Auch ich führe den größten Teil meiner Malereien in dieser Technik aus. Ich bin mir sicher, dass dieses Buch einen kleinen anspruchsvollen Beitrag dazu leisten kann, Ihrer Liebe zum Hobby oder Beruf Porzellanmalerei mit noch mehr Freude und Enthusiasmus nachzugehen. Wie immer wünsche ich Ihnen dazu viel Erfolg!

Andreas Knobl, im September 2003

g, in this manner as well. I also do a greater
art of my other paintings in this technique too.
am certain that this book will contribute a
ttle more towards you achieving a higher
andard and for you to pursue the love of
our hobby, or your porcelain painting profes-
on, with more enjoyment and enthusiasm. As
ways, I wish you every success.

ndreas Knobl, September 2003

— *Abb. 8–10 Paradiesvögel aus der aktuellen Porzellaneier-Kollektion des Ateliers. Hier arbeiten oft mehrere Maler zusammen.*

— *Ill. 8–10 The birds of paradise series – works from the studio's current egg collection. A combined effort involving several painters often all working together.*

The work place,

the correct ergonomics and a few tips to make your work better

During my seminars, it came to my notice that many students had developed several bad habits which led to negative tendencies to what would otherwise be a good technique and high quality of work. This can already begin with the positioning of your body when you paint. It is, for example, extremely important that you are not hunched over your work table too much, as this can result in getting stiff muscles and eventually lead to back troubles. I notice, over and over again, that when people are painting freehand, they stretch out the little finger of their right hand and use this as a support and, at the same time, try to do brush strokes on the porcelain – a thing which is rather impossible to do! The arm is quite without any form of support, and even the most experienced person could not keep his hand steady! They also hold the object which they are painting far too loosely in their left hand, as there is nothing available to support it on. One ought to get out of this habit as soon as possible.

So, how can we make the work easier for ourselves?
The best thing you can get yourself is a speci arm rest, just like many painters do and, incidentally, most of the factories do too – and not without reason!
You can put some soft material on the edge the open part of the arm rest, which will be

Der Arbeitsplatz,

die richtige Ergonomie und einige Tipps zum besseren Arbeiten

Durch meine Seminare bin ich bei vielen meiner Schüler auf diverse falsche Angewohnheiten aufmerksam geworden, welche eine gute technische und qualitative Arbeit negativ beeinflussen. Das beginnt schon bei der Körperhaltung. So ist es beispielsweise außerordentlich wichtig, dass Sie niemals zu tief über den Tisch gebeugt arbeiten, denn dann sind Verspannungen und Rückenprobleme vorprogrammiert. Beim Freihandmalen sehe ich immer wieder, dass viele ihren kleinen abgespreizten Finger der rechten Hand nutzen, um sich auf dem Porzellan abzustützen, und dabei gleichzeitig versuchen, einen Pinselstrich zu ziehe – ein Ding der Unmöglichkeit! Der Arm ist hierbei ja völlig ohne Auflage und so kann auch der größte Könner seine Hand nicht ruhig halten! In der linken Hand liegt das Porzellan meist zudem viel zu locker, da auch hier kei ne geeignete Auflage vorhanden ist. Diese Angewohnheit sollte man dahe schnellstmöglich ablegen.

Wie also können wir uns die Arbeit um einiges erleichtern?
Legen Sie sich ein Malpult zu, wie es schon viele Maler und eigentlich fast alle Manufakturen nicht ohne Grund benutzen.

The bench, or arm rest, should be between 15–20cm high, depending on the actual height of your normal work table. The working surface area of this structure should have the same depth as the table itself and measure between 60–80 cm in width. These measurements allow enough space for all the necessary oil containers and paint palettes to be right in easy reach of your hand. Your arm just has to move at a 90 degree angle and all the paints, oils and the porcelain to be worked on are easily more accessible and this will make your work much more efficient. Now that your right arm is positioned on top of the bench, your body will now have a relatively upright and a less tiring sitting position.

more comfortable for your painting hand. The porcelain can then be held in your left hand and be brought over to your right hand with ease. The ball of your right hand is always placed on top of the bench (your elbow as well) and only your fingers protrude over the edge when you are painting.

Only large items (such as big vases and picture plates) which cannot fit under the cut out part of the bench, have to be placed on an easel on top of the table, and you paint using an extra moveable hand rest to work from.

Mein Tipp:

Das Malpult sollte eine Höhe zwischen 15 und 20 cm abhängig von der Höhe des Arbeitstisches haben. Die Arbeitsfläche des Pultes darf so tief sein wie der Tisch selbst und eine Breite von 60 bis 80 cm aufweisen. So haben Sie genug Platz, um alle notwendigen Ölgefäße und Farbpaletten perfekt zu platzieren, und können mit Ihrem Arm in einem 90°-Winkel alle relevanten Farben, Öle und das zu bemalende Porzellan bequem erreichen und somit rationell arbeiten! Da der rechte Arm sich auf dem Malpult befindet, wird so eine relativ gerade und ermüdungsfreie Sitzposition gewährleistet.

— *Abb. 11 Mein Arbeitsplatz. Bestes Licht bieten Neonröhren mit Tageslichtcharakter. Noch idealer ist es, wenn Sie zusätzlich ein Fenster über dem Arbeitsplatz haben.*

— *Ill. 11 My work place. The best light to work under is a "day light" neon strip light, with the addition of a window above the work place as well.*

The handling of the brush

Many students hold the brush far too low down the handle, and therefore they can only make short strokes and wobbly lines, and also their painting radius is greatly reduced. It is not possible to achieve nice long continuous strokes as the brush has to be constantly lifted up and set down again.

By holding the brush in the correct position, one has the option to either paint thick lines (putting more pressure on the brush) or thinner ones (less pressure). This action can now be achieved in both directions because you have a wider radius to work in.

My tip:

When holding the brush, the distance between the fingers and the point of the bristles ought to be between 8–10 cm. This will give you a wider radius to work in, and, if necessary, you can put more pressure on the brush which will, in turn, enable you to change direction more easily without having to actually turn the piece you are working on. That also means that you can move the brush away from you too.

An der offenen Seite des Malpultes können Sie eine weiche Unterlage an den Rand des Pultes legen. Hier lässt sich bequem die Hand auflegen. Das Porzellan halten Sie ruhig in der linken Hand und bringen es stets in die richtige Position zu der den Pinsel führenden Hand. Diese befindet sich immer mit dem Handballen auf dem Pult, genau wie der rechte Ellenbogen. Nur die Finger bewegen sich über das Pult hinaus.

Beim Malen von sehr großen Vasen oder Bildplatten, die nicht unter den Pulteinschnitt passen, ist eine Tischstaffelei mit einer beweglichen Handauflage zu bevorzugen.

Die Haltung des Pinsels

Da der Pinsel von vielen Schülern viel zu weit unten gehalten wird, sind nur kurze und wacklige Linien möglich, und der Arbeitsradius ist sehr beschränkt. Es sind keine schönen langen Pinselstriche möglich, da man permanent neu ansetzen muss.

Bei richtiger Pinselhaltung hat man die Option, Pinselstriche durch entsprechenden Druck dick und bei nachlassendem Druck wieder dünn zu zeichnen. Das kann man in jede gewünschte Richtung mit vergrößertem Radius ausführen.

Mein Tipp:

Der Abstand von den Fingern, die den Pinsel halten, bis zur Pinselspitze sollte zwischen 8 bis 10 cm betragen. So hat man einen großen Arbeitsradius und kann den Pinsel je nach Wunsch breit drücken und dabei bequem während des Malens die Richtung ändern, ohne das Motiv drehen zu müssen. Das heißt auch, dass man den Pinsel von sich weg bewegen kann.

quipment and materials

Ve basically use two different types of paint rushes. Each type of brush has a selection of fferent sizes and each size is used for a speci- purpose. A most important factor is that e bristles must be of the highest quality. The st brushes available, are those made from berian squirrel hair. The small fine liner brush made exclusively of the hair from the ani- al's neck.

Short pointed brushes

These are brushes which are capable of holding a lot of paint, and you are able to cover large areas quite evenly with them. They are also used for the initial laying down of paint and for painting over areas which are already painted. They can be used in any direction, and depending on how much pressure you put on the brush the bristles can either be flattened out like a fan, turned flat on their side or, of course, kept in a point. When they are fanned

out, they are especially useful for the delicate colour transitions and the detailed parts (e.g. the fluffy breast feathers of the birds).

Long pointed brushes

They are able to make smooth strokes in whichever direction you want to paint, and go back to their good original pointed shape afterwards. They are wonderful for painting long feathers and leaves, using just one brush stroke.

Die Arbeitsmittel

Vir benötigen grundsätzlich zwei rten von Pinseln. Jede hat eine Reihe on verschiedenen Größen, um den nterschiedlichsten Herausforderun- en gewachsen zu sein. Wichtig ist erbei, dass es sich um Kielpinsel mit öchster Haarqualität handelt. Die ochwertigsten Pinsel sind aus Feh- aar (dem Fell eines Eichhörnchens us Ostrussland). Die kleinen feinen eichenpinsel sind ausschließlich aus em Nackenhaar dieser Tiere.

urze und spitze Pinsel

ie zeichnet aus, dass man mit ihnen hr viel Farbe auf größere Flächen leichmäßig auftragen kann. Außer- em eignen sie sich für das flächige nlegen und Überarbeiten. Man kann e aufgefächert, auf der Kante und atürlich mit der Spitze malend mit nterschiedlichem Druck in jede Rich-

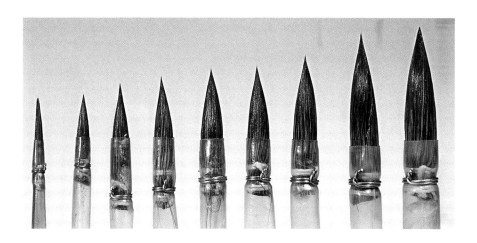

tung einsetzen. Für sehr weiche Über- gänge und Details (z.B. in den plüschi- gen Brustfedern der Vögel) sind sie im aufgefächerten Zustand ideal ver- wendbar.

— *Abb. 12 Diese Pinsel der Serie 1 (Ori- ginalhaarlänge 6–18 mm) sind für Tiere, Blumen und flächiges Anlegen und Ausarbeiten geeignet.*
— *Ill. 12 These brushes from the series 1 (original length of hair 6–18 mm) are used for painting animals, flowers and also for laying on larger areas as well.*

Preparing the brush

I always look very carefully at any new brush I buy to see if there are any bristles which are not correctly set in the ferrule. Should this be the case, I remove them with a sharp scalpel. I also cut off the very point of any new smaller liner brushes, so that I am able to work in any direction. (This is described in detail in my book "Prächtige Miniaturen/Beautiful Miniatures".) Washing out your brushes is done with either turpentine or methylated spirits/denatured alcohol. To extend the life of the brushes, they ought to be stored in a little metal box and put on top of a cloth in the box which has been saturated in clove oil. Your brushes will give you many hours of pleasure if you look after them well!

Brush handles

These should not be too short (at least 16 cm long), so that you can not only hold them bet- ween your fingers, but the brush should also "sit" in your hand, enabling you to create a steady and confident brush stroke comfortab

The palette knife

You should use one which is not too big and, above all, one which is cut diagonally at the ti and not one which is rounded, so that you ca grind the paint better and push it to the required position.

— *Abb. 13 Pinsel der Serie 2 (Original-haarlänge 9–20 mm): die perfekten Alleskönner, ideale Zeichner und Aus-arbeiter*

— *Ill. 13 Brushes from the series 2 (original length of hair 9–20 mm): the perfect all-pur-pose brushes, ideal for outlining and filling in*

Lange und spitze Pinsel

Sie folgen der Handbewegung geschmeidig »in jede Richtung« und gehen mit ihrer guten Spitze immer wieder in die Ausgangsposition zurück. Auch lassen sich lange Feder und Blätter wunderbar in nur einem Arbeitsgang anlegen.

Vorbereitung der Pinsel

Zuallererst schaue ich mir immer die neu gekauften Pinsel sehr genau an, o sich nicht doch ein paar falsch einge- bundene Haare darin befinden, und entferne diese mit einem scharfen Skalpell. Bei kleineren Zeichenpinsel kappe ich die Spitze, sodass ich besser in alle Richtungen arbeiten kann. (Di ist sehr detailliert in meinem Buch »Prächtige Miniaturen« beschrieben.

Das Reinigen der Pinsel kann in Ter- pentin oder Spiritus erfolgen. Damit sie lange ihre Qualität bewahren, soll- ten Sie sie am besten in einer kleinen

A white porcelain tile
or mixing the colours

prefer to use this to grind my colour on, as
can see (or control) the consistency of the
aint more easily on an intense white back-
round. I am also able to see the intensity of
hy colour better than on a glass palette be-
ore I start to paint.

Once the colour has the right consistency,
I then dip the brush into the centre of the
paint (because the outside could possibly have
dried up) and take so much paint out and
place as much as I need on another new porcelain tile.

Very important:

*This other tile should never be used to
grind your colours on! The reason being
that when you grind the paints, any scrat-
ches on the tile will be so sharp as to bad-
ly damage the hairs on your brushes when
you pick up the paint later. Your brushes
will be short lived and it will also spoil the
quality of your painting.*

Metalldose auf einem mit Nelkenöl
etränkten Lappen lagern. So haben
ie lange Freude an Ihren Pinseln.

Pinselstiele

Diese sollten nie zu kurz sein (Länge
nindestens 16 cm), da sie nicht nur von
en Fingern gehalten werden, sondern
uch noch in der Hand liegen sollten,
m so eine ruhigere Pinselführung
cherzustellen.

Farbspachtel

Hier sollten Sie einen nicht zu großen
yp verwenden und auf alle Fälle
inen, der vorne abgeschrägt ist und
icht rund, da sich die Farbe damit
equemer aufspachteln und an die
ewünschte Position schieben lässt.

Porzellanpaletten

Diese verwende ich bevorzugt zum
ufspachteln, da auf dem intensiv
eißen Untergrund die Konsistenz
er Farbe gut zu sehen und zu kon-
ollieren ist. Auch erkenne ich im

Gegensatz zu einer Glaspalette besser,
welche Intensität meine Farbe gerade
hat, bevor ich zu malen beginne.
Ist die Farbe im gewünschten Zustand,
so tauche ich mit der Pinselspitze in
das Zentrum der Farbe (denn außen
kann sie schon wieder etwas einge-
trocknet sein) und bringe so viel Farbe,
wie ich zum Malen gerade benötige,
auf eine neue Porzellanplatte auf!

Ganz wichtig:

*Diese Platte sollte niemals zum Auf-
spachteln der Farben verwendet
worden sein! Denn durch das Spachteln verursachte Kratzer sind so
scharf, dass sie die Haare des Pinsels
beim Farbeaufnehmen arg beschä-
digen können. So verringert sich die
Lebensdauer des Pinsels, und es lei-
det die Qualität Ihrer Malerei.*

Painting mediums and making your own fat oil

Making your own fat oil is the old, well-established process of evaporating turpentine. You put turpentine into a fairly tall vessel, so that any colour that comes out of the brush can sink to the bottom and the remaining turpentine on top, keeps clean. This is then placed into a more shallow vessel which will eventually collect the evaporated fat oil. Once the process starts, the fat oil is produced automatically if you keep the taller vessel constantly topped up to the rim with fresh turpentine. The newly evaporated fat oil "creeps" over the edge and is collected in the shallow vessel beneath.

My tip:

Using your own fat oil has the advantage that it harmonizes well with the other oils you use and also when you are actually painting. Your colours do not "bubble", flake or have other changes of character and colour after firing as could happen if you use "open" oils or other artificial fat oils.

Die Ölzucht und die Malmedien

Hier bietet sich am besten die altbewährte Ölzucht an, mit einem etwas höheren Gefäß für das Terpentin, damit sich die vom Pinsel abfallende Farbe am Boden gut absetzen kann und das Terpentin somit sauber bleibt. Dieses Gefäß steht in einer flacheren Schale für das Dicköl, welches sich – ist die Ölzucht einmal eingerichtet – automatisch neu bildet, wenn das Terpentingefäß täglich bis zum Rand nachgefüllt wird. Ein Teil des Terpentins »kriecht« bekanntermaßen als nun dickeres Öl über den Rand in das untere Gefäß.

Mein Tipp:

Selbst gezüchtetes Dicköl bewirkt beim Malen eine größere Harmonie zwischen den Ölen und somit auch bei Ihrer Malerei! Auch kommt es damit nicht zum Aufkochen, Abplatzen und anderen Veränderungen der Farbe nach dem Brand, wie es bei der Verwendung von offenen oder auch künstlichen Dickölen passieren kann.
Das ist sehr wichtig, da meine Malereien ohne Zwischenbrände gearbeitet werden, die Farbe an dunklen Stellen schon sehr kräftig liegt und nicht abplatzen darf. Das geschieht auch nicht! Es sei denn, Sie übertreiben und malen schwärzer als Schwarz. Auch hier haben Farblagen Grenzen. Aber eigentlich bekommt man sie ohne Probleme in dieser Technik immer so dunkel, wie man sie benötigt.

This is very important as in my method of painting (without any firing in between), I lay on the colours very strongly and therefore they should definitely not flake off at all. This will not happen! It could be that you want to exaggerate and paint blacker than black, and even here the layers of colours have their limits, but actually with this technique you do not have any problems, you can paint as dark as you need to.

The turpentine which you use must definitely be pure balsam turpentine which has not been refined or rectified/distilled, otherwise it spoils the manufacturing of good fat oil. When you first start to make your own fat oil, you have to start off the process by using a fat oil which has originally been evaporated from the same turpentine which you normally use for your painting; both oils should be in harmony with each other.

The medium 1 is the name which I have given to the only other medium which I use to grind the colours with. It is really nothing more than a mixture of oil of cloves and lavender oil, and serves the purpose of keeping the colours workable for a longer period.

Important: Only use the medium 1 for the first painting!

as Terpentin sollte unbedingt ein rei-
es Balsamterpentin sein, welches
cht gereinigt und rektifiziert ist.
um erstmaligen Einrichten der
Izucht sollte man unbedingt ein
icköl verwenden, welches aus dem
erpentin hergestellt wurde, das man
ch zum Malen benutzt, denn die bei-
en Öle müssen harmonieren.

as Medium 1 ist von mir so benannt,
es das einzige zusätzliche Medium
t, welches ich zum Beimischen ver-
ende. Es ist nichts weiter als eine
ischung aus Nelken- und Lavendelöl
d dient zum Verlängern der Mal-
higkeit der Farbe.

Wichtig: Es darf nur für die flächige Anlage der Farbe verwendet werden! Würde man das Medium 1 bei der Überarbeitung eines Motivs auf der ungebrannten Farbe verwenden, so würde der Untergrund aufgemalt. Je größer die anzulegende Fläche ist, desto mehr Medium 1 gebe ich bei. Nachteil: Je mehr Medium beigegeben wird, umso mehr, das werden Sie merken, lässt die Fähigkeit nach, die Farbe dunkel malen zu können. Also nehmen Sie nur so viel als nötig.
Das sind Erfahrungswerte, die Sie während des Arbeitsprozesses bei den Trockenphasen Ihrer Farbe kennen lernen werden.

If you use this medium 1 when you paint on top of unfired colours, you will succeed in removing the first colour you laid down. The larger the surface to be painted, the more medium 1 is mixed with the ground colours. Disadvantage: The more medium 1 you mix in, you will notice that it will be more difficult to paint that particular colour any darker later on. So only put in as much as is necessary. Experience will teach you about the time it takes each colour to dry while you are working with them.

— Abb. 14–16 Studien zu Lora, einem hellroten Ara
— Ill. 14–16 Studies of Lora, a Scarlet Macaw

Transferring the design onto the porcelain

Make your design to the size that you want with the help of a photocopier. Turn over the paper and firmly scribble all over this side with a special chinagraph pencil used for drawing on porcelain or glass and then rub this into the paper with a cloth using quite a bit of force.

Important: This should be done very thoroughly so that no little crumbs of graphite

Übertragen der Vorlage auf das Porzellan

Bringen Sie die von Ihnen ausgewählte Vorlage mit Hilfe eines Kopierers auf die gewünschte Größe. Die Rückseite der Kopie mit einem Porzellan- oder Glasmalstift kräftig einreiben und dann mit einem Tuch unter hohem Druck verreiben.

Wichtig: Sie sollten dies sehr ordentlich ausführen, sodass keine Rückstände (Krümel) des Bleistifts mehr zu sehen sind. Denn diese würden sich so auf das Porzellan mit übertragen. Sie sind extrem störend beim Malen und lassen ein sauberes Arbeiten nicht zu. Das Porzellan reibe ich vorher mit einem in Spiritus (Alkohol) und Terpentin getränkten Lappen ein und poliere dies wieder mit einem trockenen Tuch. So bleibt ein zarter, unsichtbarer Film auf dem Porzellan, der uns die nötige Haftung und die Feinheit der Linien garantiert.

are visible, otherwise these will be transferre onto your porcelain as well. These little lump are extremely irritating when you are painti and do not allow your work to have a "clear appearance. Before transferring the design, I rub over the porcelain with a cloth dipped methylated spirits and turpentine first and then polish it over again with a dry cloth. Th leaves a very thin film on the porcelain whic then guarantees that only the very finest of lines are transferred. You affix the photocop (graphite side down) onto the porcelain and

Dann fixiert man die Kopie (Graphi schicht nach unten) auf dem Porzella und fährt mit einer Pausnadel die wichtigen äußeren Linien des Vogels den Schnabel, das Auge und die Federn des Flügels nach. Aber nur di se nachzeichnen, die eine ganz klare Rahmung aufweisen.

Auch wichtig: Übernehmen Sie nur ganz wenige und unbedingt notwend ge Details im Bereich Kopf und Hals (aber nicht im Brustgefieder), da Ble stiftspuren jeder Art beim flächigen Anlegen sehr störend sind! Sie sollten auch gleich zu Beginn des Aufpausens kontrollieren, dass die Linien nicht zu dunkel werden. In di sem Fall bitte den Druck beim Auf- pausen reduzieren, so werden die Li en heller. Wenn die Linien fast nicht zu sehen sind, ist es ideal.

ace over only the most important details ith a tracing needle – such as the outline of e bird, the beak, the eyes and the wing athers. But only trace those details which eed a clear definition.

lso important: Only trace a few of the really mportant details on the head, throat and reast feathers because any unnecessary gra- hite lines are very irritating when you come put down your first layer of paint. ght at the beginning, you should check the

intensity of the traced lines, and make sure that they are not too prominent. If they are too dark, just reduce the pressure on the tracing needle and the lines will be lighter – ideally, the lines ought to be barely visible.

Mixing (grinding) the colours

I use about 60% turpentine and 40% fat oil for mixing the paint and it should be ground together so that no lumps of powder remain visible at all. If you still see some, then continue to grind in a circular motion adding more

pressure on the palette knife. I then push this into a heap and it should "run" just a little bit, but then stop. Should the colour dry out too quickly, simply add a small amount of fat oil to it, on the other hand, if it is too oily, then add a little more colour powder and turpentine and grind once more.

As I mentioned before, when I need to cover a larger area, then I add a few drops of medium 1 so that the mixture keeps workable for a lon- ger period.

)as Anmischen (bzw. nspachteln) der Farbe

Iier verwende ich ca. 60% Terpentin nd 40% Dicköl. Die Farbe sollte so ut aufgespachtelt sein, dass keine arbklümpchen mehr zu sehen sind. alls doch, die Farbe unter hohem)ruck mit dem Spachtel in kreisenden ewegungen weiter bearbeiten. Dann hiebe ich sie zu einem Haufen, sie arf noch etwas nachgeben (breit lau- n) und sollte dann aber stoppen. Soll- beim Malen die Farbe zu schnell ein- rocknen, gibt man einfach noch etwas Dicköl zu. Wird die Farbe im Gegen- atz zu fettig, so spachtele ich etwas ehr Farbpulver und Terpentin zu. Vie schon erwähnt, füge ich bei der nlage von größeren Flächen ein paar ropfen Medium 1 bei, um die Farbe nger malfähig zu halten.

Vichtig: Nicht vergessen, bei der Aus- rbeitung neue Farbe anzuspachteln, lls Sie mit Medium 1 gearbeitet haben.

Ebenso wichtig: Immer genug Farbe für die zu malende Fläche aufspach- teln. Wenn während des Malens nach- gespachtelt werden muss, kann es pas- sieren, dass dann die Farbe der Malerei schon angetrocknet ist. Ganz abgese- hen von der Tatsache der sich schneller verschlechternden Qualität der Farbe und dem ständigen Neuanmachen.

Fehlervermeidung: Niemals mit dem Pinsel in eine angetrocknete Farbe gehen, sondern die Farbe immer aus der Mitte der frisch angespachtelten Farbmenge entnehmen. Es sollte auch nicht auf einem schon einmal benutzten Teil der Palette gear- beitet werden, auch wenn sich nur Öl oder Terpentin darauf befindet. Der Pinsel bleibt sonst hängen, verklebt, seine Beweglichkeit wird einge- schränkt. Deswegen bitte immer da- rauf achten, dass die Paletten sauber sind und die Farbe frisch ist.

Important: Do not forget that when you are painting in the details later, mix up fresh colours (without medium 1), if you have used medium 1 in the first painting.

Equally important: Always grind enough paint ready for the area to be covered. If you have to stop half way through and mix some more paint – it can happen –, then your first colours have dried. Apart from anything else, stopping work to grind more paint means extra work for you.

Avoiding mistakes: Never put your brush into paint which has dried out, always pick up paint from the middle of the heap of ground colour. Your brush should not be put on to any part of the tile which has been used for anything else before, even if it has had just oil or turpentine on it. Your brush will have the tendency to be caught and stick on the tile and its manoeuvrability will be limited. So I remind you, please, always keep your mixing palette clean and your paints nice and fresh.

Preparing the brush before loading it with paint

1 I take some of my own fat oil out of the container and put it on my mixing palette. Then I dip the base of the bristles (those close to the ferrule) into the fat oil and twist it around so that enough oil is in the base – remember, just the base! I then tak a clean and lint-free cloth and carefully

Das Präparieren des Pinsels vor der Farbaufnahme

1. Ich entnehme Dicköl aus der Ölzucht und bringe es auf meine Malpalette auf. Dann tauche ich den hinteren Teil des Pinselkörpers in das Dicköl und drehe ihn darin, um genügend Dicköl – wohlgemerkt nur im hinteren Teil der Pinselspitze – zu haben. Nun entferne ich vorsichtig auf einem nicht fusselnden Lappen Dickölreste aus der Pinselspitze (dieser Lappen sollte sich immer in der Nähe der Paletten befinden).

2. Nun tauche ich den Pinsel bis knap zur Hälfte in Terpentin, gehe auf meine Malpalette und bewege ihn unter leichtem Druck in einem gro ßen Radius aus dem lockeren Hand gelenk heraus hin und her. (Der Pinsel sollte dabei einen Aufsetz winkel von ca. 45° haben.)

So vermischen sich die beiden Öle in der Mitte des Pinsels und geben ihm die gewünschte Beweglichkeit und Harmonie. Er sollte sich nun spielend leicht hin und her bewegen lassen. Das Dicköl bewirkt außerdem, dass die Farbe schön gleichmäßig aus dem Pinsel läuft, dass er sich wunderbar breit drücken lässt und während des Malens sogar sehr schöne Richtungs wechsel möglich sind. Es kann Ihre Arbeit enorm erleichtern.

remove any excess oil from the rest of the bristles.

Then I dip (roughly) the half of the bristles in turpentine, put it on my palette and gently move it back and forth in a circular movement (the brush should be at an angle of about 45 degrees).

ou have now mixed the two oils in the mid-le of the brush and this will give you the de-red manoeuvrability and harmony – it should

be very easy to move the brush gently back and forth. The fat oil has the ability to let the paint flow from the bristles evenly, allowing the bristles to spread out beautifully and permitting you to change the direction of the brush very nicely. It can make your work so much easier.

Important: Never completely dip the whole of your brush into the paint, just take it up to the half of the bristles (maximum).

During painting, regularly check your brush to see if it has the correct amount of oil in it and, if necessary, repeat the preparation process once more.

Here you have two pictures, one is how a properly prepared brush should look when it is flattened out on the palette, and the other one is how it should not look – these pictures are useful to you for controlling the consistency of the painting medium on your brush.

Wichtig: Bei der Farbaufnahme nie-als mit dem Pinsel komplett in die arbe eintauchen. Man nimmt maxi-al die Farbe nur bis zur Hälfte in den insel auf.

ährend des Malens sollte man regel-äßig die gerade beschriebene Aus-ewogenheit der Öle im Pinsel kon-ollieren und wenn nötig wieder her-ellen.

nbei sehen Sie zwei Abbildungen, ie der Pinsel aussehen sollte und wie icht, wenn man ihn auf der Palette uffächert, um die Konsistenz der almittel zu kontrollieren.

— *Abb. 17 Dieser Pinsel ist unpräpariert, das heißt, er ist nicht mit genügend Ölen versehen. So ist kein geschmeidiges Arbeiten möglich.*
— *Ill. 17 This brush is not well prepared, which means that there is not enough oil in it. It is not possible to perform smooth brush strokes.*

— *Abb. 18 Hier dagegen sehen Sie einen Pinsel im Idealzustand. Erst jetzt sollten Sie Farbe aufnehmen.*
— *Ill. 18 You can see that this brush, however, is in an ideal condition. Only now is it ready to receive paint.*

Practical exercises with the brush for painting the plumage

I notice at my seminars, that everyone wants to start painting straight away. It is often the case that students are not aware of the most important basic rules of holding the brush, and rarely have they been told how this is done. Before I paint any subject, it is important that I work out where I ought to place my brush in order to start correctly. For example – do I want to paint a continuous thick or thin line all in one stroke and in any direction as well, or painting an area which changes from a light to a darker colour? You should be able to lay on uneven layers of paint as well as perfectly smooth layers in every direction – and that means painting away from yourself as well! Once you have mastered using your brush, your work will be twice as easy, quite apart from the results being better. If you want to achieve good results quickly, practising exercises like these should not be underestimated!

Step 1: Gather a lot of paint in the tip of your brush, fan out the bristles and paint from left to right until there is no more paint – just oil coming from the bristles.

Step 2: Do the same as in illustration 1, but first making a stroke curving to the left, then downwards finally ending up turning to the right. Take more colour on your brush and paint a second darker coloured layer under the first feather you painted. Start at the left side and pull the colour downwards. Repeat

Pinselübungen zum Malen des Federkleids

Bei meinen Seminaren sehe ich, dass alle gerne sofort mit dem Malen beginnen wollen. Oft wissen die Schüler aber wichtigste grundsätzliche Dinge über das Handling des Pinsels nicht und sind anscheinend zuvor selten darauf hingewiesen worden. Bevor ich an ein beliebiges Sujet gehe, ist es wichtig, dass ich meine Pinsel richtig einsetzen kann, um beispielsweise eine lange dünne oder dicke Linie gleichmäßig zu ziehen, und zwar in jede beliebige Richtung, oder um Flächen von Hell nach Dunkel anzulegen. Auch sollten Sie mit und ohne Struktur in jede Richtung, das heißt auch von sich weg

— *Abb. 19 Farbübungen mit dem breiten Pinsel (siehe Beschreibungen im Text)*

— *Ill. 19 Practising with colour on a wide brush (see the instructions in the text)*

...is over and over again and you then have the impression of realistic plumage.

Step 3: Here, for example, the outer edge of the plumage is painted in whereby I put pressure on the brush and go from right to left, slightly tilting the brush and finally finishing in an upwards movement. You can see the changing directions of the strokes which avoids the end result appearing too boring!

Step 4: Push the brush down quickly and briefly, then, at a certain angle, moving it away from you at the same time. This will give the impression of the feathers laying on top. Half way down the rows of feathers change direction and paint from the top to the bottom, this also helps to prevent a "monochrome" colour effect.

Step 5: Practising simple brush strokes: start painting with the bristles in a pointed shape, push down to widen them out, pulling the brush towards you at the same time, now change direction and finish with an upward stroke.

Step 6: Laying on a smooth area of colour: your brush should be broadly fanned out and you paint from top to bottom. Now go over the same area very lightly (without any pressure) with your fanned out brush, but this time painting from left to right. This gives you different structural effects.

...malen können. Wird diese Pinselführung beherrscht, fällt das Malen doppelt so leicht, ganz abgesehen von dem besseren Ergebnis. Übungen wie diese sind also nicht zu unterschätzen, wenn Sie bald gute Erfolge erzielen möchten.

Schritt 1: Streichen Sie mit viel Farbe in der Spitze des breit aufgefächerten Pinsels von links nach rechts den Pinsel aus: den Druck währenddessen erhöhen, bis nur noch das Öl aus dem Pinsel kommt. Zwischendurch sollte der Pinsel wieder neu aufgefächert werden, ohne aber neue Farbe aufzunehmen.

Schritt 2: Machen Sie dasselbe wie bei Schritt 1, doch mit einer ersten schwungvollen Bewegung nach links, dann nach unten und rechts außen. Neu Farbe aufnehmen und eine zweite malerische Ebene mit einem dunklen Drucker unter der ersten Feder legen von links nach rechts und dabei die Farbe zur oberen Federgruppe schieben). Beginnen Sie von links, die Farbe nach unten zu streichen. Dies wiederholen Sie immer wieder, und so entsteht der Eindruck eines lebendigen Federkleids.

Schritt 3: So wird beispielsweise die äußere Abgrenzung des Federkleides gemalt, indem ich den aufgefächerten und leicht gekanteten Pinsel aufdrücke und ihn von rechts nach links bewege und ihn wieder nach oben abhebe. Auch hier sehen Sie die wechselnden Strichrichtungen gegen optische Langeweile!

Schritt 4: Drücken Sie den aufgefächerten Pinsel kurz und schnell auf und bewegen Sie ihn dabei von sich weg und kanten ihn etwas; so entsteht etwa die Silhouette einer darüber liegenden Feder. Bei der Hälfte der Feder die Richtung wechseln und von oben nach unten arbeiten. Auch das hilft gegen ein eintöniges Aussehen.

Schritt 5: Einfache Druckerübungen: Den Pinsel mit der Spitze voller Farbe ansetzen, breit drücken, ihn dabei zu sich ziehen, die Richtung wechseln und nach oben abheben.

Schritt 6: Die Anlage einer gleichmäßigen Fläche: Den breit gefächerten Pinsel von oben nach unten bewegen, dann kreuzen Sie diese Fläche, indem Sie diese von links nach rechts mit dem breit gefächerten Pinsel ohne Druck weich überstreichen. So heben sich die verschiedenen Pinselstrukturen auf.

The first outlines/loading the brush

I always begin by outlining the eyes, the beaks and the claws using brush sizes 1–3 from the series 2 (ill. 13). Having perfectly prepared the paints and the brushes as I have told you before, I dip the brush into the fresh colour and transfer it to the painting palette. I then move the brush back and forth, twisting the brush between my fingers at the same time, so that the paint is equally distributed. Then, holding the brush nearly at a vertical position (slightly slanted), I begin to draw the outline without any pressure at all. The paint almost leaves the brush by itself, the brush stroke is kept constant and I can work in any direction that I want to.

This first outline should be extremely thin, and is, more or less, used only as a guide-line (border-line) when laying down the first painting. It keeps both the inside and outside of the subject clearer and you need not worry too much about where you are painting once you have a line to follow. Once the outline is dry, this helps to stop your first painting going over it borders.

Tip: The actual outline of the bird's body is n outlined as this comes automatically when yo do the first painting.

The first painting

The preparation of the brush is the same as i is for outlining and, as I have already mention ed, a little medium 1 is added to the paint

Die erste Zeichnung

Ich beginne immer mit dem Zeichnen der Augen, des Schnabels und der Krallen und verwende dabei von der Pinselserie 2 die Größen 1 bis 3 (Abb. 13). Sind wie zuvor ausführlich beschrieben Farbe und Pinsel perfekt vorbereitet, gehe ich mit dem Pinsel in die frische Farbe und nehme mir etwas auf die Malpalette. Ich bewege die Pinselspitze in der Farbe hin und her und drehe den Pinsel dabei zwischen den Fingern, um sie im Pinsel schön gleichmäßig zu verteilen. Dann beginne ich mit dem Pinsel fast senkrecht (leicht schräg) zu zeichnen und übe dabei keinen Druck aus. So kommt die Farbe fast von ganz allein aus dem Pinsel, die Strichstärke bleibt gleich, und ich kann in jede beliebige Richtung arbeiten. Die erste Zeichnung sollte superdünn erfolgen, denn es sind mehr oder weniger nur Hilfslinien (Begrenzungen), um später die Anlage innerhalb und außerhalb der Zeichnung sehr sauber und ohne Hektik an die Linien heranarbeiten zu können. So hilft die (getrocknete) Zeichnung auch, die Farbe an den Linien stoppen zu lassen.

Hinweis: Die äußere Form des Vogels wird nicht vorgezeichnet. Sie entsteht dann automatisch während der Anlage.

Die Anlage

Die Pinselvorbereitung erfolgt wie auf Seite 12 beschrieben. Schon erwähnt habe ich, dass bei großen Flächen etwas Medium 1 zugegeben wird (aber nur in der Anlagefarbe).

Wir verwenden hier die Pinselserie 1 (Abb. 12) und je nach Größe der zu behandelnden Fläche wählen wir die passende Pinselgröße. Haben wir die Farbe auf unserer Malpalette, sollten wir für große Flächen den Pinsel mit leichtem Druck auffächern, hin und her bewegen, vorsichtig in die Farbe schieben und nur so viel aufnehmen, wie wir benötigen. Es ist logisch, dass wenn ich viel Farbe aufnehme, ich gleich richtig dunkel anlegen kann. Gehe ich nur mit der gefächerten Spitze in die Farbe und bewege den Pinsel auf meiner Malplatte etwas hin und her, sind sehr helle Anlagen möglich. Mit aufgefächertem Pinsel kann ich auch hochkant und somit in spitze Ecken hinein arbeiten. Diese Art der Pinselführung sollten Sie etwas trainieren. Natürlich lässt er sich auch ganz normal mit der Spitze arbeiten und breit drücken. So entstehen schön Drucker.

Bevor ich den Pinsel auf dem Porzellan aufsetze, mache ich so genannte »Luftübungen« über der Malerei, indem ich den Pinsel genau in die Richtung bewege, in welche ich maler will (in ständiger Wiederholung), und nähere mich immer mehr meinem Objekt. Erst wenn ich sicher bin, setze ich den Pinsel auf und bewege ihn mi mehr oder weniger Druck, gefächert oder geschlossen in die gewünschte Richtung.

Abb. 20 Die zwei Vasenobjekte mit tropischen Vögeln sind eine Gemeinschaftsarbeit des Ateliers. Die Pflanzen im Hintergrund sind mit der Airbrushpistole überspritzt und rücken so optisch weit nach hinten. Die Hintergrundfarbe ist Dunkelgrün mit wenig Schattiergrün abgetönt.

Ill. 20 The two vases with tropical birds are combined works done by several painters from the studio. The plants in the background are sprayed over with an airbrush, which optically pushes them right to the rear. The background colour is Dark-Green and shaded with a little Shading-Green.

when covering larger areas (but only in the first painting!).

Here we are using brushes from the series 1 (ill. 12) and choose the appropriate size according to the area to be painted. We have the colour on the painting palette and as it is to be used on a larger area, we gently put pressure on the brush to fan it out, move it back and forth, carefully put it in the colour and load only as much paint as we need. It is logical that when I load a lot of paint on my brush, I can lay a darker colour on to the surface. And, likewise, if I only dip the point of the brush in the colour, move it back and forth on another painting palette to remove some of the colour, the first painting will be relatively paler.

A brush which has been fanned out, can be put on edge and any narrow pointed areas can be filled in. You have to practice a bit more with this way of painting. Of course, you can paint with the point of the brush as normal and flatten it out, too. This enables you to have nice brush strokes.

Before I actually lay my brush on the porcelain, do several "trial runs" in the air exactly above and in whichever direction where I will eventually put the brush down! I repeat this movement several times, getting closer to the porcelain each time and, when I am sure that I am in the right place, I lay the brush on the porcelain and paint either with or without pressure – fanned out or closed – in precisely the chosen direction. **Important:** Keep in mind the form of the bird's body when you do the first painting, making sure that you put in light and shadows at this

24

arly stage, so that it looks three-dimensional
ight from the beginning. Please lay on as much
 the first painting as you can!
 doing this, I can save painting over it too
ten which would not be beneficial to its final
uality – the finished painting appears so
uch clearer.

My tip:

*Try not to play around with the colour too
much, you will only end up shoving it here*

Vichtig: Bitte beachten Sie beim An-
gen, dass Sie immer schon auf die
örperform des Vogels zuarbeiten und
n durch gezielten Einsatz von Licht
nd Schatten bereits früh plastisch
rscheinen lassen. Bitte die Anlage
hon so weit wie möglich treiben!
o erspare ich mir ein wiederholtes
Jbermalen, was auch der Qualität
icht zuträglich wäre. Die Malerei
rscheint so viel klarer.

and there until it eventually becomes dry,
and then you do have a problem!
Please do not go over paint which has only
had a few minutes drying time, wait until it
is completely dry otherwise you will destroy a lot of your previous work.
After it has dried properly, the colour ought
to have a velvety sheen to it and then you
are able to paint over it much easier. On
the other hand, if it is too oily, the colour
will run; or if it is too dry, the colour will be
picked off again.

Mein Tipp:

*Nicht lange in der Farbe herumma-
len, man schiebt sie letzten Endes
nur herum, sie trocknet, und es gibt
ein Problem.*
*Bitte gehen Sie außerdem nicht noch
einmal auf eine vor ein paar Minu-
ten gemachte Anlage, sondern warten Sie bis zur vollständigen Trocknung. Sie könnten sonst viel von
Ihrer Malerei zerstören.*
*Nach dem Trocknen sollte die Farbe
samtig schimmern, so lässt sie sich
auch besser übermalen. Ist sie dagegen zu fettig, würde beim Übermalen die Farbe breit laufen. Ist sie zu
trocken, reißt sie während des
Malens ab.*

My tip:

*When I am painting large areas, I never
set the brush down again directly next to
the straight stroke which I have just made,
but place the brush just a little bit over the
stroke which I have just painted. I then
avoid getting a "wooden-panel-look" and
achieve a nice evenly structured surface.
It is a good thing to be able to get into a
rhythm – start in one corner and paint in
a consistent manner.*

Mein Tipp:

*Wenn ich Flächen anlege, setze ich
nie den Pinsel neben der Fläche auf,
die ich gerade gemalt habe, sondern
werde immer noch einmal über
einen Teil der gerade gemalten
Fläche gehen. So vermeide ich einen
»Dachziegeleffekt« und bekomme
schöne gleichmäßig strukturierte
Flächen.*
*Gut ist, wenn Sie generell bei der
Anlage schon zu Ihrem Rhythmus
finden, an einer Ecke anfangen und
ihn dann konsequent durchziehen.*

Abb. 21, 22 Details der Vasen
Ill. 21, 22 Details of the vases

Filling in/the second painting

The brush technique is exactly the same as it was for the outlining and the first painting.
I use both types of brushes for this work, the outliner from series 2 (ill. 13) for the details on the wings, beaks and claws; and the flat shader from the series 1 (ill. 12) for the softer second painting and glazing.
The colour should be freshly ground again to make sure that there is no medium 1 in it (only turpentine and fat oil should be used).

Generally speaking, the paint can be just a fraction oilier than before which allows the brush to move more smoothly. Only if the lines and details are to be very distinct can you paint more on the dry side, which then prevents the colour from spreading out – it stays where it should be!

Important: Never paint over the same part twice with your brush when doing the second painting until it is completely dry, otherwise you will pick off the colour again. Once it has

dried, there will be no problem to paint over once again. In other words – only apply more wet paint to a dry painted surface.
The paint is able to take more than one layer on top of another without giving you any trouble when firing. The reason for this, as I have said before, is in the type of oil I use. Further information regarding outlining, first painting and filling in, will be detailed later on in the step-by-step instructions.

Die Überarbeitung

Die Pinseltechnik ist dieselbe wie bei der Zeichnung und Anlage beschrieben. Ich verwende hier alle beiden Arten von Pinseln, die Zeichner der Serie 2 (Abb. 13) für Detailarbeiten, wie in den Flügeln, Schnäbeln, Krallen, und die Anleger der Serie 1 (Abb. 12) für die weicheren Überarbeitungen und Lasuren.

Die Farbe sollte hier neu aufgespachtelt werden, auch um sicherzugehen, dass kein Medium 1 an der Farbe ist (nur Terpentin und Dicköl verwenden!).
Generell darf bei der Überarbeitung etwas fettiger ausgearbeitet werden, so läuft der Pinsel geschmeidiger darüber. Nur bei dunklen Details und Linien, die sehr scharf zu sehen sein sollen, arbeitet man etwas trockener aus, sodass die Farbe nicht breit läuft und auf der Anlage gut stehen bleibt.

Wichtig: Gehen Sie während der Übermalung mit dem Pinsel nie zweimal auf dieselbe Stelle, sonst malen Sie die Farbe auf. Sobald sie aber trocken ist, ist es kein Problem, erneut darauf zu malen. Man arbeitet also generell nur auf getrockneten Farben.
Die Farben vertragen problemlos mehrere Lagen übereinander, ohne beim Brand Ärger zu machen. Dies liegt natürlich wie schon erwähnt auch an den Ölen. Weitere Hinweise zur Zeichnung, Anlage und Ausarbeitung gebe ich zu den einzelnen Beispielen der Schritt-für-Schritt-Darstellungen.

Why I do not fire between each painting

There are many reasons for painting over un-fired colours, and I will tell you just a few of them (not without intention do the famous manufacturers work without firing in between each layer).

velvety, dry first painting helps:
- to draw the new fresh colour out of the brush, as there is a certain absorbency to the undercoat and each application allows you to get a darker shade of colour.
- the brush to be steered more accurately (it does not slip to the side), which is most helpful when the brush is flattened out and you have to change direction.
- to see all the details so beautifully clearly, which is difficult to achieve after a piece has been fired, painted again and then dried once more.

Just like any other painter, I often have the problem when I am painting over a surface whereby only one part has been fired and the other part has just been dried. The fired part hardly absorbs any paint at all, whereas the unfired (but painted and only just dried) absorbs much more. In that second when my brush has contact with the dried colour, it "pulls out" three times as much paint and the brush strokes are then very difficult to control. Not only that, but I need additional time to finish my piece if I fire in between each application of colour.

Another reason, which ought not to be under-estimated, is that when you paint over unfired

Warum ich nicht zwischenbrenne

Es gibt sehr viele Gründe, auf der angebrannten Farbe zu arbeiten, von denen ich aber nur ein paar aufzählen möchte (nicht ohne Grund arbeiten die bekanntesten Manufakturen ohne Zwischenbrände).

Die samtige trockene Anlage hilft:
- die Farbe aus dem Pinsel zu ziehen, da eine gewisse Saugfähigkeit des Untergrundes vorhanden ist und jeder Anwender somit gleich viel dunkler arbeiten kann.
- den Pinsel sehr souverän zu führen (er rutscht nicht weg), und gerade beim Breitdrücken mit Richtungs-wechseln ist das hilfreich.
- alle Details der Malerei wunderbar zu erkennen, was bei einer gebrann-ten, übermalten und getrockneten Malerei viel schwieriger ist.

Allerdings tritt hier das Problem auf, dass es mir wie jedem anderen Maler auch beim gleichzeitigen Überlasieren

— *Abb. 23 Ein weiteres Beispiel unseres Ateliers mit einem Paradiesvogel-Motiv (vgl. Seite 7)*
— *Ill. 23 Another bird of paradise motif from our studio (s. page 7)*

— *Abb. 24– 26 Vorder- und Rückseite einer sehr harmonischen Vase, welche mit aufwendiger Malerei versehen ist und durch den Einsatz der Airbrushtechnik für den Hintergrund einen enormen dreidimensionalen Charakter bekommt. Hier ist das Farbenspiel im Wasser besonders gut gelungen. Eine Auftragsarbeit für das Atelier.*

— *III. 24– 26 Front and rear of a vase showing great harmony. Together with lavish painting and the background painted with the airbrush technique, a wonderful three-dimensional character has been achieved. The coloured reflections in the water have turned out particularly well. This was a commission for the studio.*

colours, you are training yourself to have total command over your paint brush when you work. You are virtually forced to figure out what to do first, before you start to paint. But what do I do if I make a mistake, you are thinking? Have no fears on that score, just keep in mind all the important tips in this book, and the number of mistakes which could happen will be greatly reduced. By the way, professionals make enough mistakes when their thoughts are not "on the job" just for a second or so!

von übermalten und nicht übermalten Stellen passiert, dass auf der nicht übermalten Stelle kaum Farbe angenommen wird. Sobald ich aber auf die Übermalung komme, »zieht« es mir die Farbe doppelt so stark aus dem Pinsel. Das ist alles schwer zu kontrollieren, ganz abgesehen davon, wie viel Zwischenbrände (Zeit) ich benötige, die Malerei fertigzustellen!!
Ein weiterer nicht zu unterschätzender Grund, auf ungebrannten Stellen zu arbeiten, ist, dass Sie Ihre eigene Souveränität in der Pinselarbeit trainieren. Sie sind quasi gezwungen, wirklich zu überlegen, bevor Sie zu malen beginnen. Und wenn Sie sich »vermalen«, denken Sie? Keine Angst! Beherzigen Sie die vielen wichtigen Tipps im Buch, dann wird sich die Zahl möglicher Fehler stark verringern. Außerdem: Auch Profis machen oft genug Fehler, weil sie in einem winzig kleinen Moment nicht bei der Sache waren.

er firing, I decide what the next step is ng to be – shall I just indicate a few details ought I to cover an area completely again?

few comments on using an rbrush

se an airbrush exclusively for backgrounds, t to give the picture more harmony and also give it a three-dimensional effect. In addi- n, I am able to get a tremendous brightness d brilliance with this technique.

All the painted and fired parts are covered with a water-soluble masking fluid/resist and then sprayed. After drying completely, the masking fluid can be peeled off like a piece of film.
Warning: When using an airbrush, you should always work in a room with an extraction fan in operation and you must wear a face mask too.

ach dem 1. Brand entscheide ich nn in der Folge, ob noch ein paar etails betont werden müssen oder ne Fläche noch etwas überlasiert wer- en muss.

in paar Bemerkungen zum irbrushverfahren

h verwende die Airbrushtechnik aus- hließlich für den Hintergrund, um m Ruhe und Harmonie sowie eine reidimensionalität zu geben. Mit ihr reiche ich zudem eine gewaltige euchtkraft und Brillanz. ie zuvor gebrannte Malerei wird mit nem wasserlöslichen Lack abgedeckt, nn wird gespritzt und der Lack, der ch nach Trocknung wie eine Folie erhält, wird abgezogen. orsicht: Airbrush sollte man nur nter einem Abzug und mit einer eigneten Atemschutzmaske ein- tzen.

— *Abb. 26 Detail Entenpaar*
— *Ill. 26 Details of a pair of ducks*

carlet Macaw

rst painting (ill. 27)

arting with the fine outline of the beak in llow-Brown and the important parts of the e as well as the black point of the eye, I con- de by painting in the red parts with Flower- d. I fill the brush with a lot of paint and start top of the head and pull the colour from e inside outwards with the broadly fanned t brush. By holding the brush at a slight gle, and by following the shape of the head,

the feathers appear to stand up as they do in reality.

I have to constantly put fresh colour on the brush, otherwise I would loose too much paint and then the first painting would appear too pale. On the upper "ruff" of the macaw I very carefully mix Orange and Yellow together. As you well know, you must bear in mind the fact that Yellow always takes the upper hand when mixed in this colour combination. In other words, you should optically paint more on the

red side. You can see distinctly on the fired picture of the macaw (see ill. 30) how the Yellow consequently stands out later again.

Now continue painting the rest of the body in Red. The wings we will leave free at this stage as each individual feather has to be painted separately and the Yellow-Orange colour must be integrated later when necessary. Take care that every feather appears really three-dimensional at this point. The wing feathers (below left) are Dark-Blue and Green, and they should

Hellroter Ara

nlage (Abb. 27)

eginnend mit der feinen Umzeich- ng des Schnabels in dessen Farbe Gelbbraun) und mit der wichtigen ugenpartie sowie dem schwarzen ugenpunkt, lege ich im Anschluss s Rot (Blumenrot) an. Ich nehme viel arbe in den Pinsel auf, fange oben am opf an und ziehe die Farbe von innen ch außen mit dem breit gefächerten insel. Durch eine etwas kantige Pin- stellung und durch das Arbeiten mit der Kopfform« entstehen die hönen, wie aufgestellt wirkenden edern.

Dabei muss ich immer wieder neue fri- sche Farbe aufbringen. Ansonsten würde ich zu viel Farbe verlieren, und dann würde die Malerei in der Anlage zu hell wirken. Am oberen »Halskra- gen« des Aras mische ich wohlgemerkt sehr vorsichtig schon etwas Orange und Gelb zu. Wie Sie ja aus Erfahrung wissen, gewinnt das Gelb bei solchen Mischaktionen immer die Oberhand. Also sollten Sie optisch etwas röter malen. Sie sehen auf dem gebrannten Ara-Bild (Abb. 30) übrigens gut, wie das Gelb später wieder hervorkommt.

Nun wird der Körper mit Rot weiter gemalt. Den Flügel lassen wir noch frei, da hier jede Feder einzeln ange- legt wird und, wo es notwendig ist, das Gelb-Orange mit integriert wird. Ach- ten Sie hierbei darauf, dass jede Feder schon recht plastisch erscheint. Die Flügelfedern links unten sind dunkel- blau und grün. Diese Farben werden gleich so dunkel wie möglich angelegt. Der Schnabel bekommt eine gelbbrau-

Abb. 27–31 Die Erarbeitung des Motivs »Hellroter Ara«
27: Anlage
Ill. 27–31 Working through the stages of painting the Scarlet Macaw.
27: First painting

be laid on as dark as is possible now. The beak has a Yellow-Brown layer which can either be integrated with the darker part now or later. This darker colour is made with Chocolate-Brown to which a little Black has been added. At first, all colours are painted with generous brush strokes from the head to the tip of the beak, leaving sufficient white showing through. Now cross over these brush strokes and work on the curvature of the beak. To do this you use a fanned out shader brush (series 1) which has been prepared properly with the medium, as I have already explained, and take it very gently (without any pressure) over the painted area. You have now given the beak a smooth texture and structure.

Filling in the details (ill. 28)

Now we will paint all the rest of the red feathers, beginning at the head once again and pulling downward until the bottom. I use Flower-Red for the light value, Dark-Red for the middle value and Rust-Brown for the darkest value. Whenever you want to shade Red, please use neither Black nor Brown if you want t

ne Anlage, in welcher auch gleich der konsequente Übergang zum dunkleren Teil stattfindet. Dieser wird mit einem mit Schwarz abgetönten Schokoladebraun erreicht.

Arbeiten Sie zunächst alle Farben in großzügigen Druckern vom Kopf weg zur Schnabelspitze hin und lassen Sie genug Weiß stehen. Nun kreuzen Sie diese Drucker und arbeiten mit der Wölbung des Schnabels. Hierfür benutzen Sie einen weit aufgefächerten Anleger (Serie 1), der gut mit den schon erwähnten Medien vorbereitet ist, und führen ihn sehr weich, ohne Druck, über die Malerei. So bringen Sie Ruhe und Struktur hinein.

Erste Überarbeitung (Abb. 28)

Jetzt malen wir die gesamten roten Federstrukturen und beginnen am besten wieder am Kopf und ziehen erneut bis unten durch. Ich verwende

28

ep it a brilliant colour. The beak has to be
...aded in a darker colour, and the lighter parts
...e just left untouched.
...he main area of the eye is painted in Light-
...reen, adding Egg-Yellow and a little Orange
...certain parts. I start first by painting the area
...ound the eye with Pale-Blue and Light-Tur-
...uoise, followed by a light wash of Shading-
...llow mixed with Yellow-Brown, and making
...re that the cheek remains the lightest part.

Continuing the painting (ill. 29)

Before the first firing I paint several deep shadows in the red feathers with Red-Brown to achieve an even more darker colour. Then finally, to get the green effect on the feathers, I apply Dark-Green and then I have added a little outlining colour for the darker parts. The blue and the green feathers have been painted over with a very intensive layer of Dark-Blue and Green.

Filling in the details of the eyes is made by using Shading-Green and a little matt outlining colour. The Yellow, done in the last step, is now painted over with Orange and Shading-Yellow. I painted around the eye very meticulously: first of all I had to paint the little folds of skin very delicately and then shade these very thoroughly with a mixture of Shading-Yellow and Chocolate-Brown. To make the area around the eye more life-like, I put in white highlights in the eye itself, on the cheek and on

Blumenrot, für mittlere Rottöne Dunkelrot und für die tiefsten Schatten Rotbraun. Bitte verwenden Sie für Rotschattierungen kein Schwarz oder Braun, wenn die Farbe ihre Leuchtkraft erhalten soll.– Der Schnabel wird nun auch dunkler gearbeitet, und hellere Strukturen werden einfach stehen gelassen.
Das Auge ist in Hellgrün mit der Farbe Eigelb und etwas Orange angelegt. Um das Auge herum beginne ich mit Hellblau und Türkis-Hell. Die weitere Fläche um das Auge lasiere ich leicht mit einer Mischung von Schattiergelb und Gelbbraun, achte aber darauf, dass die Wange der hellste Bereich bleibt.

Zweite Überarbeitung (Abb. 29)

Vor dem ersten Brand male ich noch einige kräftige Schatten mit Rotbraun ins rote Gefieder, um noch mehr Tiefenwirkung zu bekommen. Zu guter Letzt setze ich die grünen Effekte auf das Gefieder (ich habe dafür Dunkel-

grün benutzt und habe etwas Zeichenfarbe für die dunkleren Bereiche zugegeben). Die blauen und grünen Federn werden sehr intensiv übermalt (in Dunkelblau und Grün).
Die Augenausarbeitung erfolgt mit Schattiergrün und etwas Zeichenfarbe matt. Das Gelb des letzten Arbeitsschritts wird mit Orange und Schattiergelb übermalt. Um das Auge herum begann nun eine besondere Fleißarbeit: Zunächst musste ich die Hautfältchen fein zeichnen und dann sorgfältig schattieren (mit einer Mischung aus Schattiergelb und Schokoladebraun). Um dem Auge noch mehr Lebendigkeit zu geben, setzte ich weiße Lichtpunkte ins Auge, auf die Wange und die Federn unter dem Schnabel. Ein perfekt ausgearbeitetes Auge ist ein nicht zu unterschätzendes Element für die Wirkung eines Vogels. Es ist außerdem allemal interessanter, wenn das Tier in die Richtung des Betrachters schaut.
Auch der Schnabel selbst bekommt als abschließender Punkt noch ein paar

- *Abb. 30 Im entsprechenden Rahmen wirkt das Motiv noch lebensechter.*
- *Ill. 30 In an appropriate frame, the motif appears still more true-to-life.*

the feathers under the beak. A perfectly painted eye is the part of the bird which should never be underestimated. It is particularly more interesting when the bird is actually looking directly at the observer.

The beak itself now gets its finishing touch by receiving a few raised areas, which adds to it looking extremely natural.

Completion of the motif after the second fire (ill. 30)

The background is now painted with an airbrush. Above all, I chose colours which would be the most effective next to most predominant colours on the bird itself, in this case Blue and Green. These colours showed a very beautiful and a colourful luminosity even whe I intensely sprayed Black directly next to and above them. With this coloured background and the whole painting set in a golden frame the macaw now receives another tremendou optical boost.

Höhungen und wirkt nun äußerst naturgetreu.

Vollendung des Motivs nach den zweiten Brand (Abb. 30)

Der Hintergrund wurde mit Airbrus gearbeitet. Ich wählte vor allem diejenigen Farben dafür, die schon als deut liche Effekte im Vogelgefieder enthal ten sind (Blau und Grün). Sie zeigen sehr schöne farbige Lichtspiele noch, nachdem ich intensiv Schwarz daneben und darüber gespritzt habe.

Mit diesem Hintergrund und in einer goldenen Rahmen gesetzt hat der Ara eine enorme optische Steigerung erfal ren.

— *Abb. 31 Der Ausschnitt zeigt die faszi nierende Wirkung des Auges.*

— *Ill. 31 This close up section shows the fascina ing effects of the eye.*

Black-capped Parrot

First painting

This parrot was painted at one of my seminars. Its feathers show really wonderful colour combinations. The working procedure: sketch the eye very exactly and afterwards lay in Black and Flower-Red.

Colour the beak with different shades of Brown, which include Flower-Red, Yellow-Brown, Brown and Chocolate-Brown. The part round the eye is painted with a very thin layer of the same colours parallel to those which you just have used.

The dark head feathers are painted in Black with a little amount of Dark-Violet added to it. To get the pretty blue effect between the eyes and the beak, I apply a thick layer of Dark-Turquoise with a little Dark-Green to the upper part. For the "ruff" around the throat I begin by lightly applying Egg-Yellow in the lightest part under the eye, and continue downwards to the darker area where I add some Orange and continue with Yellow.

The white breast feathers I lay on with the brush slightly fanned out, and each stroke is made precisely in the correct position to give them a realistic appearance. So that I am able to control my brush easily and so that the finished effect is not too dark, I pick up only just enough colour on the tip of my brush which I need for each stroke (see "Practical exercises with the brush", page 20). The colours I use are: Yellow-Brown and Dark-Grey; for shading, I add a very little amount of Dark-Purple to it. By using this colour the pic-

Grünzügelpapagei

Anlage

Dieser Papagei ist in einem meiner Seminare entstanden. Sein Gefieder zeigt wundervolle Farbkombinationen. Die Vorgehensweise: Das Auge sehr genau umzeichnen, später Schwarz und ein Blumenrot hineinlegen.

Den Schnabel mit den unterschiedlichsten Brauntönen anlegen. Dazu Blumenrot, Gelbbraun, Braun und Schokoladebraun verwenden. Die Fläche um das Auge gleich parallel dazu mit den Farben der gerade verwendeten Mischung dünn mit anlegen. Die dunklen Kopffedern sind mit Schwarz und etwas Violett-Dunkel bemalt. Für den schönen Blaueffekt zwischen Auge und Schnabel trage ich gleich sehr intensiv Türkisblau Dunkel und etwas Dunkelgrün am oberen Teil auf.

Für den »Halskragen« beginne ich mit Eigelb sehr zart im Licht unterhalb des Auges, werde nach unten zu immer dunkler, füge hierfür Orange bei und lege gleich alles in Gelb an.

Das weiße Brustgefieder lege ich mit einem etwas aufgefächerten Pinsel an. Ich setze bewusste Drucker, die die Plastizität betonen und nehme bei diesem Arbeitsgang nur so viel Farbe in die Pinselspitze, wie ich wirklich benötige. So wird das Ergebnis nicht zu dunkel, und ich kann mit dem Pinsel besser spielen (siehe auch den Abschnitt Pinselübungen, Seite 20). Hierfür verwendete Farben: Gelbbraun und Dunkelgrau; zum Abtönen ganz wenig Dunkelpurpur beigeben. So bekommt die Farbe einen nicht ganz klar zu identifizierenden warmen Charakter. Bei diesem Beispiel ist es sogar gewünscht, dass die Farben in sich variieren, das verleiht dem Ganzen mehr Natürlichkeit.

ure is given just a hint of warmth without being too overdone. In this example given it was my wish that the various colours should mingle with each other to lend the whole subject a much more naturalistic appearance.

Important: Never use just Grey or Black when shading any white areas. They make the subject too cold and sombre looking.

The green wing feathers start at the top with a mixture of Light-Green going into Olive-Green, and the part underneath has Green added to it as well. The tail is done in Olive-Green with a little Yellow-Brown added to it. The colour for the claws is a mixture of a soft Purple and Dark-Red (ratio 1:1).

My tip: Generally speaking, please do show more courage to mix your own colour combinations! Try it, you can get some really good results that way.

Detailing – no need to fire extra

The beak, eye, the dark head feathers and also the claws, are painted once more in the same colours as were used in the first painting. Filling in the details on the yellow part of the throat you should apply the colour a little more strongly as it appears in reality because the red colour will "fire away" that much more.

Here we will use only a little Shading-Yellow as we still want to retain the bright orange character. So in this case we will work from "light to dark", preferably going from Orange to Flower-Red to Dark-Red, in that order.

Wichtig: Für die Schattierung weißer Flächen niemals reines Grau oder Schwarz verwenden. Es wirkt kühl und düster.

Das grüne Flügelgefieder ist oben mit einer Mischung von Hell- bis Olivgrün angelegt, nach unten ist Grün zugemischt. Der Schwanz ist in Olivgrün mit etwas Gelbbraun gehalten. Die Farbe für die Krallen ist im Verhältnis 1:1 mit zartem Purpur und Dunkelrot angemischt.

Mein Tipp: Haben Sie generell mehr Mut zum Mischen der Farben, es können sehr schöne Nuancierungen dabei herauskommen!

Ausarbeitung des Motivs ohne Zwischenbrand

Schnabel, Auge und dunkle Kopffedern sowie die Krallen werden mit denselben Farbnuancen wie diejenigen der Anlage überarbeitet. Die gelbe Ausarbeitung des Halsbereichs malen Sie am besten etwas kräftiger, als die Farbe in Wirklichkeit wäre, da gerade die rötlichen Farben recht stark »wegbrennen«.

Wir verwenden hier nur wenig Schattiergelb, um den leuchtend orangefarbenen Charakter zu erhalten. So benutzen wir in solchen Fällen vorzugsweise »von Hell nach Dunkel« die Farben Orange, Blumenrot und Dunkelrot.

Die grünen Federn werden deutlich ausgezeichnet und nach ihrer Trocknung mit der schon bekannten Mischung (Grün plus Zeichenfarbe matt) schattiert. Der Schwanz darf gleich mit derselben Farbe ausgearbeitet werden.

Zuletzt mische ich die Farbe Weiß mit etwas Weiß matt (das ist ein fast reinweißer Farbkörper), da diese noch mehr Intensität besitzt. Ich setze diese Mischung auf die weiß verbliebenen Stellen im Brustbereich und betone natürlich noch einmal besonders den Schnabel und die Augenpartien.

– *Abb. 32, 33 Grünzügelpapagei: Anlage und Ausarbeitung (Seite 40)*
– *Ill. 32, 33 The Black-capped Parrot: the first painting and filling in the details (p. 40). The green feathers are outlined quite heavily and after this colour has dried, they are shaded with the familiar mixture of Green plus matt outlining colour. The tail can also be shaded with this same colour.*
Finally, I mix White together with a little matt White (this is nearly a pure white pigment/colouring matter) which possesses more "body" to it than just plain white. I apply this mixture to the parts on the breast which had been left white in the first painting and, naturally, I emphasize the "highlights" on the beak and in the eyes once more.

— *Abb. 33 Grünzügelpapagei*
— *Ill. 33 Black-capped Parrot*

— *Abb. 34 Fertiges Bild:*
  Gelbhaubenkakadu
— *Ill. 34 Completed picture:*
  Sulphur-crested Cockatoo

Sulphur-crested Cockatoo

First painting

I lay on the first colour in the dark areas around the eye by using strong and heavy brush strokes. Now I paint every feather individually, starting at the eye and working away from it, keeping the shape of the head in mind. Only now will the contours of the head emerge when you paint in the head feathers! I do this very patiently and deliberately – that is the essence of this method of painting! Give yourself lots of time and move the brush in a slow and a decisive manner. By painting each feather one by one like this, you will move towards the lighter part and the colour will automatically get paler and paler.

Important: Do not work with the paints too dry, otherwise you will lose the soft appearance. The feathers on top of the head I paint in a half circle, with my brush completely fanned out, going in the direction of the feathers themselves. Whilst you are painting, keep in mind the structure and the direction of the feathers. When I paint the feathers underneath the eye, I put colour on just the tip of the fanned out brush and, painting from the left to the right, make a short sweeping movement and then lifting the brush off again. I begin at the top and work down, constantly making the same short brush strokes – in this way the feathers look as if they are overlapping each other nicely. The beak is shaded in Dark-Violet and Black and, as you can see, the Yellow-Brown colour is "caught up" with the shading colour and they are blended together.

Gelbhaubenkakadu

Anlage

Wie immer beginne ich mit der Zeichnung des Auges und des Schnabels. Die Anlage beginne ich direkt an den dunklen Stellen um das Auge herum und setze sehr gezielte und dunkle Drucker. Nun lege ich jede Feder des Kopfes einzeln an, starte »vom Auge weg« und achte auf die Kopfform, welche durch die Federn ja erst entsteht. Dies tue ich mit Ruhe und Bedacht – das A und O in dieser Art der Malerei, Hektik ist wirklich fehl am Platz! Lassen Sie sich Zeit, bewegen Sie den Pinsel langsam und überlegt. So setze ich nun Feder für Feder und werde ins Licht hin immer heller.

Wichtig: Nicht zu trocken arbeiten, da sonst der softe Charakter verloren geht.

Die Federn oberhalb des Kopfes male ich mit dem aufgefächerten Pinsel und lege einen Halbkreis an, welcher die Feder andeutet. Während des Malens sind die Struktur und Richtung der Feder zu beachten. Bei den Federn unterhalb des Auges benutze ich den Pinsel mit etwas Farbe in der aufgefächerten Spitze, bewege ihn von links nach rechts, drücke ihn kurz schwungvoll auf und hebe wieder ab. Ich beginne von oben nach unten zu arbeiten und wiederhole die Pinseltechnik stetig. So entstehen diese sich schön überlappenden Federgruppen.

— *Abb. 34–36 Die Entstehung des Gelbhaubenkakadu. 34 (S. 41) Fertiges Bild; 35 Anlage; 36 Übermalung*

— *Ill. 34-36 The developing stages of the Sulphur-crested Cockatoo. 34 (p. 41) Completed work; 35 First painting; 36 Detailing*

I use a large size liner brush, of the series 2, to paint the yellow crest feathers because they can hold a lot of paint and, because they have long bristles, I am able to paint theses feathers in one long continuous sweeping stroke. I use a mixture of Lemon-Yellow and Egg-Yellow (ratio 1:1).

Filling in the details

This is done with the same colours which you have used in the first painting – but they are freshly ground once more, of course, but without medium 1 this time. I hardly apply any colour in the lighter parts of the feathers, as most of the colour has already been laid on in the first painting. The white colour is painted accurately on the lighter areas, so that it brings this part more to the foreground. You can see how, literally, the bird gains more plasticity. I use Shading-Yellow, together with a little Yellow-Brown, to shade the yellow feathers.

Finishing the painting after firing.

Once I have airbrushed on the background colour, the cockatoo has now got its true-to-life appearance, and really stands out from the porcelain. The background is a purple colour which gets paler towards the outside of the composition, and the dark Black-Purple area a perfect additional contrast. The fine band around the plate is done in one hundred per cent Gold paint.

Der Schnabel ist mit Violett Dunkel und Schwarz gearbeitet. Gelbbraun wird, wie zu sehen ist, gleich mit hineinlasiert.
Für die großen gelben Kopffedern verwende ich einen großen Zeichenpinsel der Serie 2, um viel Farbe aufnehmen zu können. Durch seine Länge kann ich die Federn in nur einem Arbeitsgang sehr schwungvoll anlegen. Ich mische hierfür Zitronen- und Eigelb im Verhältnis 1:1.

Übermalung

Die Übermalung erfolgt größtenteils mit den Farben der Anlage, aber natürlich neu aufgemischt ohne das Medium 1. In den hellen Ebenen des Gefieders überarbeite ich kaum noch, dies sollte alles schon mit der Anlage fertiggestellt sein. Das Weiß setze ich dann sehr gezielt, um die hellsten Stellen noch mehr in den Vordergrund zu holen. Sie sehen förmlich, wie der Vogel an Plastizität gewinnt.

Die Ausarbeitungsfarbe für die gelben Federn ist Schattiergelb, in das ich noch etwas Gelbbraun gemischt habe.

Fertigstellung nach dem Brand

Nach dem Aufbringen der Airbrush-Hintergrundfarbe hebt sich der Kakadu völlig lebensecht von dem Porzellan ab. Der Hintergrund ist purpurfarben und nach außen heller gehalten, sodass der dunkle Schwarz-Purpur-Rand noch einen perfekten Zusatz-Kontrast abgibt. Die gelben Federn schauen bewusst über diesen Rahmen hinweg, so scheint das Tier den Kopf förmlich aus dem Bild heraus zu drehen. Der schmale Rahmen ist aus hundertprozentigem Gold.

— *Abb. 36 Übermalung*
— *Ill. 36 Detailing*

Gelbbrustaras

Anlage

Es wurden folgende Farben verwendet: Für die Köpfe Gelbgrün, für den Schnabel des oberen Vogels Schwarz mit etwas Purpur und Gelbbraun abgetönt; das blaue Federkleid mit Türkis Dunkel, und die hellen Stellen unter den Federn sind eine Mischung von Orange und Purpur. Die gelben Federn sind mit Eigelb und Orange, der Ast ist mit Gelbbraun, Rot und Braun gemalt.

Der gesamte Hintergrund zeigt eine Abtönung von Grau in Richtung Blau und Grün. Hier sind der Fantasie keine Grenzen gesetzt.

Golden-collared Macaws

First painting

I have used the following colours: Yellow-Green for the head; Black for the beak of the upper bird, with the addition of a little Purple and Yellow-Brown for shading; Dark-Turquoise for the blue plumage and a mixture of Orange and Purple for the light areas under the feathers. The yellow feathers are done in Egg-Yellow and Orange, the branch is painted in Yellow-Brown, Red and Brown. The whole of the background is shaded in a grey colour with hints of Blue and Green – but here your own imagination can run free!

— *Abb. 38 Übermalung*
— *Ill. 38 Second layer*

Outlining the plumage

We use Dark-Turquoise and to this you can add any amount of matt outlining colour that you think is right, and outline every feather very precisely. The outline of the head is done in Olive-Green mixed with a little matt outlining colour. The Egg-Yellow area which has already been put on previously, is now shaded with Shading-Yellow, Red and Yellow-Brown. The branch now is painted over with Brown and Chocolate-Brown.

Painting over the first painting again

Once the outlines of the feathers have dried, I put in the shadow areas with Turquoise-Blue and shade this with outlining colour in the darker regions. I work on the beak now and give more emphasis to the yellow area by adding Yellow-Brown and Dark-Red to give it more depth.

Zeichnung des Federkleids

Hier verwenden wir Türkis Dunkel. Mischen Sie je nach Bedarf Zeichenfarbe matt dazu und umzeichnen Sie jede Feder sehr genau. Die grüne Kopfzeichnung ist in Olivgrün mit etwas Zeichenfarbe matt gehalten. Das bereits angelegte Eigelb wird mit Schattiergelb, Rot und Gelbbraun ausgearbeitet. Den Ast überlegen Sie mit Braun und Schokoladebraun.

Übermalung

Ist die Federzeichnung getrocknet, lege ich mit Türkisblau die Schatten an und töne diese in den dunkleren Regionen mit Zeichenfarbe ab. Ich arbeite die Schnäbel aus und gebe dem Gelb noch mehr Betonung, indem ich mit etwas Gelbbraun und Dunkelrot mehr Tiefe hineinarbeite.

Ausarbeitung

Nachdem ich das Bild – erstmals – gebrannt habe, habe ich die Vögel und den vorderen Ast mit wasserlöslichem Lack abgedeckt. Mit der Airbrushpistole sprühte ich einen recht hellen diffusen Hintergrund auf (mit Grau, welches mit Hellgrün und Hellblau abgetönt wurde). Nachdem der Hintergrund gebrannt ist, lasierte ich abschließend noch ein paar Schatten ein, um dem Vogelmotiv mehr Ruhe und Plastizität zu geben.

— *Abb. 39 Ausarbeitung*
— *Ill. 39 Filling in the details*

lling in the details

ter the picture has been fired for the first
ne, I covered the bird and the branch in the
reground with water-soluble masking fluid,
d I airbrushed the background really lightly
h a hazy mixture of colours – using Grey,

I then added Light-Green to it in some areas
and Light-Blue to it in others. After the background has been fired again, I finally put in an
extra wash of colour over the shadow areas,
which keeps the area around more peaceful and
this will make the bird motif stand out more.

— *Abb. 40–43 Detail des Gefieders. O*
  ginalmaß der Platte: 13 x 18 cm
— *Ill. 40–43 Details of the feathers. Original*
  size of the plate: 13 x 18 cm

40   41   42

Black-cheeked Lovebird and Fisher's Lovebird

It was my basic idea to plan an exciting theme, and to bring as many of these pleasant little birds of the same species into the picture as I possibly could. It was my intention to show these birds in as many different aspects as possible – all very lively and very three-dimensional – and place them in front of a very quiet background.

The onlooker is supposedly in the centre of all this activity, as most of the birds are cheekily looking at him directly out of the picture. One is actually peeping through its open wing tips! I deliberately placed the tail feathers of the Fisher's Lovebird, flying into the picture (above right), in front of the open wing feathers of the black-cheeked Lovebird, which as well just wanted to land. This bird is painted quite faintly which gives more depth to the scene.

Because there are so many birds to see in the picture and all at different angles, I will now explain to you how to paint each and every one of them.

Ideas for composing pictures

Before we are able to start, we should have made tracings of all the birds onto the porcelain. The plants in the whole of the picture are painted freehand, and as suitable examples for

Schwarzköpfchen und Pfirsichköpfchen

Bei diesem Bild war es meine Grundidee, möglichst viele dieser sympathischen Vögel einer ähnlichen Gattung (in diesem Fall Agaporniden aus Afrika) in ein spannungsvolles Bildkonzept einzubringen. Ziel war es auch, sie in den vielfältigsten Bewegungen vor einem ruhigen Hintergrund sehr lebendig und dreidimensional darzustellen.

Der Betrachter ist dabei im Zentrum des Geschehens, denn die meisten Vögel schauen frech aus dem Bild heraus direkt auf ihn. Einer lugt sogar durch seine geöffneten Flügelspitzen. Das rechts oben einfliegende Pfirsichköpfchen setzte ich bewusst mit seinem Schwanzgefieder vor den weit geöffneten Flügel des ebenfalls gerade landen wollenden Schwarzköpfchens. Dieses ist etwas blasser dargestellt, um die Tiefenwirkung zu erhöhen.
Da die Vögel in so vielfältiger Bewegung zu sehen sind, möchte ich Ihnen die Erstellung jedes Einzelnen nicht vorenthalten.

Ideen zur Bildkomposition

Bevor wir beginnen können, sollten wir die Vögel aufgepaust haben. Die Pflanzen des gesamten Bildes werden frei aufgezeichnet. Als Vorlagen für die Hintergründe und Beiwerk eignen

- *Abb. 44 Schwarzköpfchen und Pfirsichköpfchen im Silberrahmen*
- *Ill. 44 Black-cheeked and Fisher's Lovebirds in silver frame*

— *Abb. 45 Anlage: Gut sieht man hier bei diesem Einzelporträt, wie bereits in der Anlage die Federstrukturen am Kopf sowie das zugemischte Orange im Brustbereich deutlich sichtbar sind. Das links neben dem Vogel befindliche Blattwerk ist mit einer Mischung von Grün und Dunkelgrau angelegt.*

— *Ill. 45 First painting: Clearly you can see in this single portrait, how well the first painting indicates the head feathers and also the mixed orange colour on the breast area. The foliage, on the left of the bird, is painted with a mixture of Green and Dark-Grey colours.*

the background and any additional foliage, good books are available on this subject. Sele material from books specializing on tropical rain forests where you can find many plants, flowers and inspiring ideas for the backgrour

Sketching

Important: Any objects which require a defi- nite outline ought to be done at the beginnir

sich besonders gut Bücher über tropi- sche Regenwälder, in denen Sie eine Vielzahl von Pflanzen, Blumen und anregenden Hintergrundideen finder

Zeichnung

Wichtig: Alle Objekte, die eine klare lineare Abgrenzung haben, sollten zuerst gezeichnet werden, denn das erleichtert die weitere Anlagearbeit! Deswegen beginnen wir als Erstes mi der Zeichnung der Schnäbel und benutzen dafür ein leuchtendes Blu- menrot. Umzeichnen Sie die Vogel- füße mit Blaugrau und tönen Sie die Krallen noch etwas dunkler ab. Das Auge wird sehr genau mit Schwarz gezeichnet und kann nach Trocknung der Farbe gleich plastisch und dunkel ausgelegt werden. Bitte den Lichtpunkt freilassen!

this will make things easier for the first
[pain]ting later. We begin, therefore, by outlining
[th]e beak in a bright Flower-Red and the birds'
[fee]t in Blue-Grey and then shade the claws
[jus]t a little bit darker.

[Th]e eye is outlined in Black with great precis-
[io]n and, after the colour has dried, it can be
[pai]nted with dark colours to make it look
[mo]re realistic – please do not forget to leave
[th]e highlight free of paint!

— *Abb. 46 Überarbeitung: Man sollte im
Gelb immer genug Licht lassen und
dort nur sehr zart die Federn andeuten.
Hier gilt der Grundsatz: Weniger ist
mehr! Denn eine schöne harmonische
Anlage kann durch eine übertriebene,
unruhige und zu dunkle Ausarbeitung
im Lichtbereich regelrecht zerstört
werden.*

— *Ill. 46 Filling in the details: One should leave
enough light in the yellow area and only just
indicate the feathers very lightly. Here the
general rule is – the less, the better! A nice
and harmonious first painting can really be
destroyed if it is too excessive or too fussy
and also if it is made to look too dark in what
should be the lighter areas.*

First painting

The feathers around the eye are painted with a very thin layer of Dark-Grey and the beak is filled in with Flower-Red – remember that any light reflections have to remain pale.

Now begin to work on the head: start painting from the beak moving towards the yellow area first with Grey, gradually going into Chocolate-Brown and, just in a few areas, you can add a little Violet for the darker parts. It is really important that you maintain the shape of the head (this means, you paint in the direction of the way the feathers lie) remembering to take into account its structure as well as indicating the light and the shadow areas.

Immediately after laying on the Chocolate-Brown, and before it is dry, we carefully apply Lemon-Yellow and Egg-Yellow (mixed together) on top. Then, just in a few areas, blend the colours together with a fanned out brush which is free of paint. Please make sure that during any further painting, the Yellow area is not discoloured by any Brown colour. A little bit of Orange is now added to the upper part of the breast area.

Now we lay a thick layer of Yellow on the breast right down to where the green part begins. We then blend the two colours together (as already instructed) and continue further, right down to the end of the tail, using several shades of Green and adding the occasional touch of Yellow.

Anlage

Die Federn um das Auge herum sind ganz leicht mit Dunkelgrau gemalt. Der Schnabel wird mit Blumenrot angelegt, und Sie sollten auch hier nicht vergessen, die Lichteffekte hell stehen zu lassen.

Weiter geht die Arbeit am Kopf, welcher mit einem Übergang von Grau in Schokoladebraun angelegt und an manchen Stellen mit noch etwas Violett abgetönt werden kann. Wir arbeiten vom Schnabel weg in Richtung gelbe Fläche. Es ist wirklich wichtig, dabei unbedingt die Kopfform mit zu betonen – das heißt, in Richtung des Federverlaufs zu arbeiten –, diese strukturell anzudeuten sowie auch Licht und Schatten zu berücksichtigen.

Gleich im Anschluss lasieren wir eine Mischung aus Zitronen- und Eigelb vorsichtig an den Ansatz, solange das Schokoladebraun noch nicht trocken ist. Bringen Sie die Farben an einigen Stellen mit einem aufgefächerten farbfreien Pinsel aneinander. Bitte achten Sie darauf, dass sich das Gelb beim weiteren Anlegen nicht mit dem Braun verfärbt. Im oberen Brustbereich mischen wir noch etwas Orange bei. Dann legen wir das Gelb der Brust schon schön kräftig bis an den Grünansatz, »vermitteln« den Übergang wie schon beschrieben und arbeiten diese Fläche bis zum Schwanzende mit verschiedensten Grüntönen unter teilweiser Zugabe von Gelb aus.

Die Pflanzenwelt wird im Vordergrund mit Mischungen aus Blumenrot, Orange, Gelbbraun und für die Blätter Gelbgrün kräftig angelegt. Zum Hintergrund hin werden wir heller, und die Farben verändern sich mehr in Richtung Olivgrün bis Blau-Grün.

he undergrowth in the foreground is made
p of a mixture which includes Flower-Red,
Orange, Yellow-Brown and the actual leaves
re done in a thicker layer of Yellow-Green. It
ets lighter as it goes further into the back-
round and the colour changes too, going
rom an Olive-Green into a Blue-Green.
he Fisher's Lovebird, one is in the middle of
he picture and another one is above right,

gives us another range of colours. We will
begin in the front part of the head area with
Flower-Red, follow by mixing a little bit of
Orange to it and paint in the direction of the
breast, where it becomes yellow. We paint the
rest of the body and continue down to the tip
of the tail with a mixture of colours which include: Yellow-Green, Green and Egg-Yellow.
The outside of the tail feathers is painted in
Middle-Blue.

The upper part of the wing is a changing spec-
trum of colours ranging through Yellow-Green,
Green to Olive-Green, and the under part of
the wing you could paint in either Air-Blue or
Light-Blue, followed by adding nuances of
Light-Violet or Yellow-Brown afterwards.

Beim Pfirsichköpfchen im Bild oben in
der Mitte und oben rechts gibt es eine
twas andere Farbwelt. So beginnen
vir am vorderen Kopfbereich mit Blu-
nenrot, mischen dann Orange bei und
gehen in Richtung Brust zu Gelb über.
Wir legen anschließend den weiteren
Körper mit einer variierenden
Mischung von Gelbgrün, Grün und
Eigelb bis in die Schwanzspitze an. Die
äußeren Schwanzfedern sind mit Mit-
elblau gestaltet.

– *Abb. 47 Fertige Malerei: Hier wird*
  sehr deutlich, wie im Gelb die Ausar-
  beitung kühler erscheint und dass sie
  auch zurückgebrannt ist. Das bedeutet
  für unsere Arbeit: Die Ausarbeitung
  auf dem Gelb immer etwas wärmer
  und dunkler anlegen.
– *Ill. 47 The finished painting: Here it is shown*
  quite distinctly how the Yellow colour appears
  cooler and that is has also faded by firing it.
  This means: when working with Yellow, always
  lay it on in a warmer and darker value.

— *Abb. 48 Anlage: Die Anlage sollte sehr
ruhige, plastische Flächen zeigen, und
gerade beim plüschigen Brustbereich de
Tiere darf sie etwas wolkiger wirken.*

— *Ill. 48 First painting:The first painting should
indicate a very calm and a three-dimensiona
area and then, particularly in the fluffy
breast section of the bird, it should appear
more indistinct.*

- *Abb. 49 Überarbeitung: Gut zu erse-hen ist, wie die Pinseldrucker mit der Kopfform »mitgehen«, wie sie im Dunklen beginnen und sich durch Aus-streichen der Farbe nach rechts im Licht auflösen. Im Grün fällt die wie schon im Text beschriebene Vielzahl von möglichen Farbnuancen auf, sie reicht vom wärmeren olivfarbenen Unterkleid bis zum kühler und dunkel erscheinenden Flügel rechts. Nur bei den linken Ausläufern der Federn des oberen Flügels werden die einzelnen Federn vor der Schattierung gezeichnet.*

— *Ill. 49 Filling in the details: It is clear to see that the brush strokes "follow" the shape of the head, note how they start off quite a dark shade and as they go to the right, the colour on the brush fades away into the light area. As explained in the text, the green part is made up of several different shades of Green. It varies from a warm Olive, on the feathers underneath, to a cooler and darker appearance to the wing on the right. Only on the left side of the plumage of the upper wing detailed feathers are being painted in before the shading.*

— Abb. 50 Fertige Malerei: Ganz wichtig wurde es hier, die Schattenbereiche weiter zu betonen, um die Plastizität zu steigern. Das trifft besonders auf die Schattenstellen unterhalb des oberen Flügels und die des Kopfes zu. Ich betonte außerdem den seitlichen Flügel noch stärker. Hinter der vorderen Kralle lässt sich durch eine dunkle Lasur auf den Federn weit mehr Tiefe erreichen. Nach dem letzten Brand ist wiederum zu bemerken, wie die Farben auf den Pflanzen kühler erscheinen. Deshalb wiederhole ich meinen Tipp für Sie, immer wärmer und leuchtender anzule gen, als es meine Vorlage zeigen kann. Als Vorteil ist zu werten, dass nach dem Brand das in der Kopfanlage dem Scho koladebraun beigemischte Violett hervorragend zur Geltung kommt. Es gibt dem im äußersten Vordergrund befind lichen Vogelkopf auch seine größtmögli che Lebendigkeit.

ainting over unfired colours

pply the next layer of paint, in exactly the me order as I did in the first painting, but ly after the paint has dried thoroughly.
emember: When you paint on unfired olours, be sure not to paint over the same ot twice otherwise you will pick up the paint ain on your brush!
he beak I paint in the most brilliant red that I ve in my palette – and that is Flower-Red. en I paint in only a few "mere suggestions"

of shadows with a darker colour, so that the beak does not loose its brightness. The head now receives some Chocolate-Brown but never, under any circumstances, adding any Black, otherwise the painting could easily become dirty looking and would loose its radiance.

I am able to make the eye appear more lifelike when I put a half circle of darker colour into it. I usually paint Shading-Yellow over the top of Yellow and tone it down in the parts which are lighter or warmer or in orange parts.

I can also add Yellow-Brown and Brown to Shading-Yellow to get a darker value.

Important: Generally speaking, blue is shaded by adding matt outlining colour to the original blue colour which you have initially used in the first painting. In light areas you add less and, accordingly add more in the shadow areas.

I use Shading-Green in the green areas, adding a lot of outlining colour to it when I need a darker shade – this gives it an enormous feeling of depth. So that the painting remains lively, I do not rigidly paint over all of the green

---

Die Flügeloberseite ist eine wechselnde arbwelt von Gelbgrün, Grün und livgrün. Die Flügelunterseite kön-en Sie mit Luft- oder Hellblau anle-en und diese Farbtöne später nuan-ert überarbeiten sowie Violett Hell der Gelbbraun beigeben.

Übermalung

rst wenn die Farbe gut durchgetrock-et ist, beginne ich mit der Überma-

lung in derselben Reihenfolge, wie ich zuvor die Farben angelegt habe.

Nicht vergessen: Nie zweimal auf die-selbe Stelle gehen, Sie malen sonst die untere Malschicht auf.

Den Schnabel überarbeite ich mit dem leuchtendsten Rot meiner Palette (dem Blumenrot). Hierbei aber nur noch im Schattenbereich ein paar dunkle Ef-

fekte setzen, damit der Schnabel seine Leuchtkraft nicht einbüßt.

Den Kopf arbeite ich mit Schokolade-braun aus und gebe auf keinen Fall Schwarz hinzu, da die Malerei sonst sehr schnell schmutzig wirken kann und ihre freundliche Ausstrahlung verliert.

Dem Auge kann ich durch einen dunk-len, halbrunden Schatten noch mehr Lebendigkeit geben. Gelb überarbeite

---

Ill. 50 The finished painting: At this stage it was important to continue to work more intensely on the shaded areas to make them more "alive". This particularly applies to the shadow part underneath the upper wing and also to the head. I also emphasized the wing on the side more strongly, as well. By applying a dark wash of colour on the feathers behind the claw in the foreground, I am able to give it more depth.
On the other hand, after the final firing, now it is more noticeable how much cooler the

colours appear on the plants. So I will repeat my tip – you should always lay on a more warm and a more brilliant value of colour than my illustrated example can show you here. A valuable advantage is that if you have mixed Violet and Chocolate-Brown together on the head area in the first painting, you see how magnificent it appears after being fired. This is able to give the greatest possible depth to the head of the bird in the extreme foreground.

— *Abb. 51 Anlage: Gut erkennbar sind
beim Kopf des mittleren Vogels die
Übergänge der Farben von Schokolade
braun zu Gelb. Beim unteren Vogel
sind die beiden Farben hart gegeneinan
der abgegrenzt verblieben.
Beachten Sie auch die Vielzahl der
Farbnuancen in der Pflanzenanlage,
welche zum Hintergrund hin immer
kühler gemalt wurden.*

— Ill. 51 First painting:On the head of the bird
the middle, it is very noticeable how the
transition from Chocolate-Brown colour goe
over to the Yellow. On the other bird below,
the two colours have a definite border-line
separating each of them.
Take note of the many different colours of
the foliage in the background area, these
should always be painted in cooler values.

Abb. 52 Überarbeitung: Das Pfirsichköpfchen (oben) wird mit Blumenrot
bis in den Brustbereich hinein ausgearbeitet. Es bekommt eine sehr zarte
Zeichnung auf den Flügelfedern (mit
Zeichenfarbe und Mittelblau. Zum
Überlasieren töne ich die Farbe mit Violett und Gelbbraun noch etwas ab.

Ill. 52 Filling in the details: The Fisher's Lovebird (above) is painted with Flower-Red right
down into the breast part of the bird. It gets
a very soft outline on the wing feathers with
outlining colour and Middle Blue. I then give
this a wash of Violet with the addition of Yellow-Brown.

63

areas, just hints of shading here and there. This can be done with Yellow-Brown, Brown, Blue and also in any other various shades of Green which you have at hand.

Everything ought to appear very soft with sweeping movements, and only here and there should some details be recognizable – and these details you make with more definite strokes of the brush. Only the wing and the tail feathers, which are clearly visible, have a fine outline around them. Wait until the outline is dry, and then you can paint over it very lightly and, where necessary, any fine structures can be accentuated and any "strong" shadows be put in.

The claws are now painted over with shades Blue and Grey to make them more effective. Lastly, I give a light wash in one or two places (not forgetting to wait until it is dry), and also put in a few dark areas as well. After completing all this, the picture is fired at a temperature of, maximum, 800°C/1472°F.

ich meistens mit Schattiergelb und töne dieses zum Teil in helleren, wärmeren und in Bereichen mit Orange ab. Dem Schattiergelb kann ich außerdem Gelbbraun und Braun beimischen, um es noch dunkler zu bekommen.

Wichtig: Blau wird generell mit der Zeichenfarbe matt ausgearbeitet, welche man aber den jeweiligen Anlagefarben beimischt. Im Licht sehr wenig und im Schatten entsprechend mehr. In der Grünüberarbeitung verwende ich häufig Schattiergrün, welches in dunklen Bereichen stark mit Zeichenfarbe abgetönt wird und so eine enorme Tiefe erzielt. Um die Malerei lebendig zu halten, wird das Grün nicht stur mit einer Ausarbeitungsfarbe durchgearbeitet, sondern noch nuancenreicher abgetönt. Dies kann mit Gelbbraun, Braun, Blau und allen vorhandenen Grüntönen passieren.

Alles wird sehr weich und schwungvoll überarbeitet, und nur hier und da sollen nuanciertere Details erkennbar sein (gezielt gesetzte Drucker). Nur die Flügel- und Schwanzfedern, die konkret sichtbar sind, werden dünn umzeichnet. Warten Sie, bis die Zeichnung getrocknet ist. Dann können Sie weich übermalen und wo nötig feine Strukturen andeuten und »kernige« Schatteneffekte setzen.

Die Krallen werden mit Blau und Grautönen noch wirkungsvoll überzeichnet.

Zu guter Letzt werde ich an verschiedenen Stellen noch etwas überlasieren (wohlgemerkt wieder nach der Trocknung) und einige dunkle Effekte setzen. Daraufhin geht das Bild in den Ofen und wird bei maximal 800 °C gebrannt.

– *Abb. 53 Fertige Malerei: Wie kleine Edelsteine leuchten nun die Vögel vor dem brillanten Hintergrund. Sie sehen, wie zurückhaltend ich in den Lichtbereichen übermalt habe. Die Schattenbereiche sind natürlich stärker übermalt worden, und so entsteht ein optimaler plastischer Eindruck.*

– *Ill. 53 The finished painting: The birds now appear to be shining little jewels in front of the brilliant background. You can see how sparingly I have painted over the lightest area. The shaded areas are, naturally, painted more strongly which gives them a very favourable three-dimensional effect.*

Airbrush

Before I start, I cover the birds and a section of the background very carefully with a water-soluble masking fluid, and spray some kind of "beams of sunlight" shining through the background. I remove the masking fluid which comes off very easily.

Be careful: Under no circumstances touch the freshly sprayed paint with anything. It lays on the porcelain just like a fine covering of dust, so you must get the piece into the kiln as quickly as possible and fire at 800°C/1472°F. Looking at the picture after firing, you notice that the birds which are in front of the colourful background now appear to be quite different to what they were when the background was white – they now seem to be much lighter. So, if necessary, colours in the areas which have "fired away", should be painted over once more.

Airbrush

Hierfür decke ich die Vögel und einen Teil des Hintergrundes sehr korrekt mit einem wasserlöslichen Abdecklack ab und sprühe dann einen lichtdurchfluteten Hintergrund mit der Airbrushpistole. Ich entferne vorsichtig den Lack, der sich wunderbar abziehen lässt.

Vorsicht: Keinesfalls die gespritzte Farbe anfassen. Sie liegt nur wie Staub auf dem Porzellan, darum sollte das Stück schnellstmöglich wieder in den Ofen wandern (800 °C). Betrachtet man nach dem Brand das Bild, stellt man fest, dass die Vögel vor dem farbigen Hintergrund ganz anders wirken als vorher auf dem Weiß und meistens heller erscheinen. So werden Stellen, die es nötig haben, und solche, die etwas »zurückgebrannt« sind, nochmals übermalt.

— *Abb. 54 Anlage: Hier beginne ich mit dem vorderen Flügel. Ich nehme viel Farbe (Olivgrün und Grün) auf, lege die großen Federn mit einem Drucker an und »vermittle« die Farbe noch etwas mit dem aufgefächerten Pinsel. Jede einzelne Federspitze wird separat angelegt. Vergessen Sie nicht, sich nach der Originalvorlage zu orientieren und die einzelnen Federn in ihrer jeweils variierten Farbigkeit zu übernehmen. Die Flügelspitzen auf der anderen Seite des Vogelkopfes werden mit Violett Hell und Hellblau angelegt.*
Sind die Flügel farbig angelegt und die Farben getrocknet, lege ich die unterschiedlichen Farben auf dem Körper des Tieres an, male ohne Pause von oben nach unten, sodass die Farbe nicht eintrocknen kann. Zwischen den gespreizten Flügelspitzen arbeite ich die Farbe sehr akkurat an die bestehende Anlage heran. Für die blauen Schwanzfedern verwende ich Hellblau.

Ill. 54 First painting: I begin by painting the wing in the front. I take a lot of colour (Olive-Green and Green) on the brush, paint the large feathers with one stroke and then "connect" the colours a little bit with the brush in a fanned out position. Each tip of every feather is painted on separately. Don't forget to constantly refer to the original example and copy precisely every colour variation of each individual feather. The tips of the wing on the other side of the bird's head are painted in Light-Violet and Light-Blue. Once the first colour has been put on the wings and then dried properly, I then continue to lay on the other different colours onto the body, painting in such a way from bottom to top without stopping so that the paint does not have a chance to dry. Very accurately, I now paint quite close to the colour of the first painting between the outstretched wings. I use Light-Blue for the blue tail feathers.

67

— *Abb. 55 Überarbeitung: Nun betonen wir die vorderen Flügelspitzen entsprechend dunkel, so heben sie sich besser von jenen des helleren Vogels unten ab. Die weiteren Deckfedern des Flügels werden mit einer ganz unterschiedlich abgetönten Zeichenfarbe matt überzeichnet (siehe Text Seite 61 ff.). Dies gilt auch für die blauen Federn.*

— Ill. 55 Filling in the details: Now we darken the tips of the wing in the front to a suitable extent which then makes them stand out from the lower bird's lighter colour. Following the written instructions in the text (see p. 61 ff.), all the other wing feathers are now outlined in various shades of matt outlining colour. This also applies to the blue feathers as well.

– *Abb. 56 Fertige Malerei: Schön hebt sich der Vogel nach dem Brand von seinem Artgenossen unten ab, welcher um einiges blasser gehalten wurde. So hat der Schwanz, der über dem Flügel des unteren Vogels schwebt, auch die doppelte Farbintensität.*

– Ill. 56 The finished painting: After firing, the bird now appears to stand out more from its other fellow Lovebird below, which still has a paler appearance. Also the tail of the bird (which hangs above the wing of the lower bird) has twice as much depth of colour.

Abb. 57 Detail des Vogelkopfes
Ill. 57 Detail of the bird´s head

Abb. 58 Anlage: Für die hinteren Deckfedern des Flügels wurde Grün verwendet, und beim vorderen Flügel wurde das Grün mit Olivgrün abgetönt. Dann wird immer mehr Violett Hell und Hellblau für den mittleren Teil zugemischt. Die großen Federn sind dann ein Mix aus allem.

Ill. 58 First painting: The rear plumage on the wings is done in Green, and the wing in the front has Olive-Green added for the shading colour. More and more Light-Violet and Light-Blue are then added to the part in the middle and finally, the large feathers are a mixture of all the colours together.

— Abb. 59 Überarbeitung: Die Ausarbeitung auf dem Körper ist sehr lebendig, aber nie gegen die Körperform oder den Verlauf der Federn gerichtet. So bleibt die Ruhe im Vogel erhalten. Wenn Sie Ihre Vögel bei der Ausarbeitung stricheln, dann geht die plüschig wirkende Leichtigkeit verloren; das Ergebnis gleicht dann mehr einem kolorierten Kupferstich. Eine solche Malweise gab es wohl in der Meissener Manufakturmalerei – es ist Geschmackssache, was Ihnen mehr gefällt: die naturechte oder die stilisierte Variante ...

— Ill. 59 Filling in the details: The details on the body are very intense, and yet they never go against the line of the bird's body or against the direction of the feathers. In this way the continuity of the bird is maintained. If you outline the bird at this stage, the light and fluffy appearance is lost and it will appear to look more like a coloured copperplate engraving. This way of painting was once popular with the Meissen Manufactory – it is certainly a matter of taste which you prefer the most – being true to nature or to have the more stylized manner.

Mein genereller Tipp:

Achten Sie stets auf die »Verlaufrichtung« der Federn, die die Form des Vogels so richtig herausheben. Also keinesfalls kreuz und quer arbeiten, sondern immer Drucker setzen.

Abb. 60 Fertige Malerei: Mein Vogel, der im Begriff ist, auf dem Ast zu landen, ist voller Lebendigkeit und Transparenz. Damit er noch besser zur Geltung kommt, habe ich den Ast links von ihm nicht abgedeckt und bei der Airbrusharbeit gleich mit überspritzt. So »geht er etwas in den Hintergrund weg« und macht dem Vogel keine Konkurrenz.

Ill. 60 The finished painting: My bird, which is just on the point of landing on the branch, is full of vigour and clarity. Just for the reason to appear more prevalent, I have not masked out the branch to its left and therefore have covered it when I airbrushed over my work. It then has the appearance of "melting into the background" and leaving the bird without any competition.

My general tip:

Always pay attention to the direction in which the feathers lie on the bird to make it look more real. In other words, do not lay your brush down any old way, but concentrate on the direction of your brush strokes.

Finches

These colourful and amusing finches look just like little jewels set in this blue coloured frieze. The birds have been placed so that the ones on the left, look to the left and those on the right, naturally look to the right. Only the white one, painted in Blue-Grey, in the center is looking directly at the spectator.

I will indicate here just a few colours which I used for the individual birds, as most of the colours I have described in detail already in the text using other examples.

Colours used

The bird, far left: head and belly: Dark-Grey and Black with a little Yellow-Brown on top; breast: Orange and going into Flower-Red towards the beak.

Second from the left: first painting: Lemon-Yellow going into Yellow-Brown; details: Shading-Yellow, adding Chocolate-Brown in the shadow areas.

— *Abb. 61–63 Prachtfinken: Anlage, Überarbeitung und Fertigstellung*
— *Ill. 61–63 Finches: First painting, filling in the details and finishing the painting*

Prachtfinken

Wie kleine Edelsteine wirken die farbenfrohen und lustigen Prachtfinken auf diesem Fries mit blauem Hintergrund. Die Vögel sind so angeordnet, dass die linken nach links schauen und die rechten natürlich nach rechts. Nur der mittlere Weiße (gemalt mit Blaugrau) schaut direkt auf den Betrachter. Ich möchte hier nur noch auf einige wenige Farben eingehen, die ich bei einzelnen Vögeln verwendet habe, denn die meisten Farben habe ich im Text bei anderen Beispielen schon ausführlich beschrieben.

Farbverwendung

Vogel ganz links: Kopf und Bauch: Dunkelgrau mit etwas Gelbbraun überarbeitet, mit Schwarz; Brust: Orange und zum Schnabel hin Blumenrot.

Zweiter von links: Anlage: Zitronengelb bis Gelbbraun; Ausarbeitung: Schattiergelb, im Schatten mehr Schokoladebraun.

Dritter von links: Kopf: Dunkelrot und überarbeitet mit Rotbraun und Schwarz; Bauch: Türkis hell und Mittelblau; Federstrukturen mit Zeichenfarbe matt.

Vierter von links: Bauch: Mit Dunkelrot sehr hell beginnen, dann über Rotbraun bis zum Schwarz hin arbeiten.

Erster von rechts: Bauch: Holzbraun und Orange, Überarbeitung: Braun mit etwas Zeichenfarbe matt.

Zweiter von rechts: Bauch: Anlage Hellblau, überarbeitet mit Türkis Dunkel und Zeichenfarbe matt; Körper: Braun und übermalt mit einer Mischung von Braun und Violett Dunkel

Dritter von rechts: Brust: Orange mit ein wenig Dunkelgrau abgetönt; Kragen: Türkis Hell und übermalt mit Türkis Dunkel.

75

Third from the left: head: Dark-Red painted over with Red-Brown and Black; belly: Light-Turquoise and Middle-Blue; details of feathers: matt outlining colour.

Fourth from the left: belly: start lightly with Dark-Red, followed by Red-Brown, going into Black.

First from the right: belly: Wood-Brown and Orange – painted over with Brown, adding matt outlining colour.

Second from the right: belly: first painting in Light-Blue, painted over with Dark-Turquoise and matt outlining colour; body: Brown, painted over with a mixture of Brown and Dark-Violet.

Third from the right: breast: Orange shaded with a little Dark-Grey; collar: Light-Turquoise painted over with Dark-Turquoise.

76

Abb. 64 Details der Vögel, Original-
röße 30 x 10,5 cm
Ill. 64 Details of the birds, original size 30 x
10,5 cm

"The enchanted prince"

As well as motifs of birds, I thought that a picture of a frog would be well received, especially as this one is such a magnificent example also found living in exotic jungles. Frogs are always a very amusing subject, even when you are choosing your motif, you have cause to feel happy! It is decorated on to one of the many porcelain eggs which we have in our special egg collection. We started off in 1990, and our large and varied collection of eggs has developed considerably since then. The egg itself is such a beautifully shaped object, which never seems to be out of date and gives perfect support to any artistic style. I have paid particular attention to the way that my frog (not only is it observing the onlooker full of self-confidence but is watching its unsuspecting prey as well!), has the correct shape and size in proportion to the egg.

I have chosen to have a tinted background in Yellow-Green so that the overall impression is one of harmony. If you hold the egg in your hand, you do not have the impression that it is made out of porcelain but, due to its transparent appearance, it looks far more like glass. While I was trying to give it a more naturalistic and three-dimensional appearance, gradually, bit by bit, I achieved this "painting-like" character. Everything is really colourful and there is hardly any white porcelain to be seen. This is certainly not a "must" for you to paint, but maybe you could try it out for yourself sometime.

›Der verzauberte Prinz«

Neben den Vogelmotiven könnte, so habe ich mir gedacht, auch ein Froschbild großen Anklang finden, zumal ein Prachtexemplar wie das gezeigte auch im exotischen Dschungel zu finden ist. Es ist in jedem Fall ein sehr lustiges Sujet, welches schon bei der Motivauswahl Freude bereitet. Es ziert eines von vielen Porzellaneiern unserer Porzellaneierkollektion, die sich seit 1990 zu beachtlicher Vielfalt entwickelt hat. Das Ei selbst ist ein so zeitloses und formschönes Objekt, dass es jede Art von Stilisierung perfekt unterstreicht. Hier habe ich sehr darauf geachtet, dass mein Frosch, der äußerst selbstbewusst gleichzeitig den Betrachter und das ahnungslose Beutetier anvisiert, in Form und Größe perfekt auf dem Ei inszeniert wurde.

Für den Hintergrund wählte ich einen grüngelben Fond, um einen harmonischen Gesamteindruck zu erreichen. Hält man dieses Ei in der Hand, hat man gar nicht mehr den Eindruck, dass es sich um Porzellan handelt. Durch seine scheinbare Transparenz wirkt es vielmehr wie aus Glas. Auf der Suche nach mehr Natürlichkeit und Dreidimensionalität im Ausdruck habe ich nach und nach zu einer solchen malerischen Charakteristik gefunden. Alles ist recht bunt, und es ist kaum noch weißes Porzellan zu sehen. Dies ist selbstverständlich kein Muss für Ihre Arbeit, aber vielleicht probieren Sie es einmal selbst.

Abb. 65 Das fertige Ei mit dem Frosch
Ill. 65 The completed egg with the frog

— *Abb. 66 Zeichnung: Die Anatomie meines Frosch-Motivs muss stimmen. Hier sehen Sie gut, wie ich für die Umzeichnung des Tieres die Farben wählte, die auch in der Anlage (Abb. 67) Verwendung finden. Die Zeichnung versteht sich als reine Hilfslinienskizze (dünn und hell) für eine akkuratere Anlage. Würde man den Frosch mit nur einer und zwar einer dunkleren Farbe zeichnen, würde dies wie ein Fremdkörper wirken – schließlich hat in der Natur auch kein Lebewesen eine lineare Umrandung! Die Pflanze legte ich ohne eine Zeichnung bereits hier farbig an.*

— *Ill. 66 Sketch: The anatomy of my frog motif has to be correct. Here you can clearly see how I chose to outline the animal in the same colours which I wanted to use for the actual painting (ill. 67). This outline (thin and pale) serves purely as a rough guide-line for the first painting. Should one use just a single colour, and a dark one at that, it would make the frog appear odd. After all, there is no creature in nature which has a solid line around. The plants I painted directly with colour without any prior outlines beforehand.*

Abb. 67 Anlage: Für den Frosch griff ich natürlich zu meiner Grünpalette mit den leuchtendsten Farben, und in das Hellgrün mischte ich sogar noch Zitronengelb, um die Leuchtkraft zu erhöhen. In den reizenden Froschfüß-chen verwendete ich zudem noch Gelb-braun. Für den Bauch des Frosches kamen diverse Nuancierungen von Gelbbraun über Türkis bis Dunkelvio-lett zum Einsatz.

In das Grün der Hintergrundpflanze mischte ich mehr gedeckte Farben wie Olivgrün, Gelbbraun und Schattier-grün, um sie vom Vordergrund besser zu separieren. Die Blüte ist Purpur und etwas Dunkelviolett.

Ill. 67 The first painting: For the frog I went straight to my selection of green paints with the brightest values, and mixed even Lemon-Yellow into Light-Green to give it that added brilliance, and in the lovely frog feet, I added some Yellow-Brown to it. For the belly of the frog I brought in several shades of Yellow-Brown and also colours ranging from Turquoise to Dark-Violet. For the plant in the background, I mixed Green with less promi-nent colours such as Olive-Green, Yellow-Brown and Shadow-Green, which makes it less prominent than the foreground. The flower is painted in Purple and a little Dark-Violet.

— *Abb. 68 Überarbeitung: An allen hel len Stellen sollte man sehr vorsichtig überarbeiten und weiche Übergänge schaffen, bevor wir die dunklen Detai mit einer Mischung von Grün und Dunkelgrün malen. Für die noch dunkleren Stellen und Schlagschatten mischte ich viel Zeichenfarbe matt in die Grüntöne. Mit einem feinen Zeich ner deutete ich dann auf dem Bauch die noppenartigen Strukturen an (Anlagefarbe). Zu guter Letzt setzte ich weiße Effekte in die Augen, auf de Bauch und auf verschiedene Körperte le, um den Körper glänzend und feuc erscheinen zu lassen (siehe das fertig gemalte Ei, Abb. 65).*

— Ill. 68 Filling in the details: In all of the lighte areas, you should be very careful when fillir in the details and be sure to make gradual colour transitions before you paint in the darker details with a mixture of Green and Dark-Green. For the areas which are even darker and for the deep shadows them- selves, I mixed a lot of matt outlining colour with the Green colours. The knobbly struc- tures on the belly I now indicated with a fir liner brush using the first colour. Then last b not least, I put in some white effects in the eyes, on the belly and on several parts of th body to give them a shiny and wet appear- ance (see ill. 65, the finished and complete painted egg).

— *Abb. 69, 70 Anlage und Überarbei- tung des Motivs »Zwei Pinguine«*

— Ill. 69, 70 The first painting and filling in the details of the "Two Penguins" motif.

Rockhopper Penguins

The composition shows a happy group of penguins. I have arranged them on a cold, clear surrounding, balanced on top of an ice-floe just before they dive into the water. I chose the rockhopper species because of their red and yellow coloured feathers which brought a bit more life into the picture, otherwise the overall impression might have been a bit too cool. Another suggestion for a motif would be to use the beautiful and gracious king penguins.

Felsenpinguine

Die Komposition zeigt eine sehr harmonische Gruppe von Pinguinen. Ich inszenierte sie in einer kühlen, klaren Umgebung, auf einer Eisscholle balancierend – kurz vor dem Absprung ins Wasser. Ich habe ganz bewusst die Gattung der Felsenpinguine gewählt, da die roten und gelben Details in ihrem Gefieder dem Bild erst Leben geben. Ansonsten wäre der Gesamteindruck vielleicht etwas zu kühl ausgefallen. Als weiteres Motiv bieten sich die schönen und graziösen Kaiserpinguine an.

Anlage

Für das dunkle Gefieder habe ich Blaugrau und Schwarz verwendet (hier ist besonders auf eine homogene, aber plastische Anlage zu achten). Der gelbe Schopf ist mit der Farbe Eigelb angelegt, und ich habe etwas Rot daneben gezeichnet. Der Schnabel: reines

First painting

For the dark plumage I used Blue-Grey and Black, paying particular attention to getting a smooth but, nevertheless, at the same time, a life-like colouring. The yellow tufts are painted first with Egg-Yellow, putting a little Red edging at the side afterwards. The beak: pure Flower-Red; white belly: Grey, Yellow-Brown and little Purple; feet: Purple and Flower-Red; ice: Dark-Turquoise and adding some Black and Grey shading to it, when necessary.

Filling in the details

To finish off the painting, I used the same colours once more on many areas which I had put on in the first painting. This gives more emphasis to the structures of the feathers and to the shadow areas, for example. On the white belly I tried to keep it looking soft as any hard structuring would destroy the "fluffy" character of the penguins' plumage. By putting extra effects in white the result is a better appearance.

After firing, I covered the penguins with water-soluble masking fluid and airbrushed the sky with Dark-Blue and the water with Turquoise.

— *Abb. 71–73 Detail Kopf*
— Ill. 71–73 Detail head

Blumenrot; weißer Bauch: Grau, Gelbbraun und ein wenig Purpur; Füße: Purpur und Blumenrot; Eis: Türkis Dunkel, und je nach Bedarf wurde es mit Schwarz und Grau abgetönt.

Überarbeitung

Ich habe anschließend mit denselben Farben der Anlage viele Stellen an den Pinguinen nochmals übermalt, um Details wie beispielsweise die Feder-strukturen und Schatten deutlich dar-zustellen. Am weißen Bauch versuchte ich, sehr soft zu bleiben, da jede harte Struktur den gewünschten »plüschi-gen« Charakter des Pinguinfells stören würde. Das Aufsetzen von weißen Effekten erhöht die Wirkung.

Nach dem Brennen habe ich die Pin-guine mit wasserlöslichem Abdecklack abgedeckt und mit der Airbrushpistole den Himmel gespritzt (mit Dunkel-blau). Für das Wasser verwendete ich die Farbe Türkis.

Abb. 74 Das fertige Bild

Ill. 74 The completed picture

Hummingbird

Little hummingbirds are quite the right subjects to have together with exotic flowers painted onto dishes and vases. I chose to have a quiet and dark background to this subject, using Purple, Violet and Black colours. The well balanced colours of these different shades gave the bird and the flower a silhouetted effect and the motif seems to rise up out of the tinted background. I used a mixture of Pink and Light-Blue for the outer border.

For the rest of the painting I have used nearly all the Green and Red paints in my palette. I added Purple and Orange to the stalk of the Strelitzia flower in the foreground and for the details in the arrangement of flowers, I used Air-Blue and Dark-Violet.

The wing of the hummingbird was made to look more alive by using a mixture of Black, Dark-Violet and Light-Blue.
The body of the hummingbird: when necessary, I added matt outlining colour to every

75

Kolibri

Die kleinen Kolibris bieten sich geradezu an, sie zusammen mit exotischen Blumen auf Schalen und Vasen darzustellen. Ich wählte hierzu einen ruhigen, dunklen Hintergrund in den Farben Purpur, Violett und Schwarz. In seiner ausgewogenen Abtönung bewirkt er für den Kolibri und die Blumen einen silhouettenartigen Effekt, die Motive heben sich wunderbar vom Fond ab. Für den äußeren Rand wählte ich eine Mischung aus Rosa und Hellblau.

Für die Malerei selber habe ich fast all Grün- und Rottöne meiner Palette benutzt. Bei der Strelitzia-Blüte im Vordergrund mischte ich noch Purpur und Orange in den Stiel. Für Details im Blütenstand verwendete ich Luftblau und Violett Dunkel.

olour I used for filling in the details. In the
reast area I put in little additional black
eathers. Once all the painting and the tinting
ith the airbrush have been completed and
he porcelain has been fired, I often paint over
ome of the details again so that the contrast
 the background and to the tinting is increas-
d to a maximum.

Der Flügel des Kolibris wurde mit
iner Mischung von Schwarz, Violett
Dunkel und Hellblau plastisch.
Der Körper des Kolibris: Für die Aus-
rbeitung habe ich jede verwendete
arbe mit Zeichenfarbe matt je nach
edarf abgetönt. Im Brustbereich setz-
 ich außerdem noch kleine schwarze
ederchen. Sobald alle Arbeiten inklu-
ve des Airbrushspritzens für den
ond abgeschlossen sind und der
rand erfolgt ist, übermale ich oft ein
aar Details, um die Kontrastwirkung
on Vordergrund und Fond zu maxi-
ieren.

- *Abb. 75–77 (S. 88) Anlage, Überar-
beitung und Fertigstellung des Motivs
»Kolibri und Blüten«*
- *Ill. 75–77 (p. 88) The first painting, filling in
the details and the finished painting of
"Hummingbird and blossoms"*

76

77

78-81 Eulen – eine Gemeinschaftsarbeit aus dem Atelier. So romantisch und schaurig schön kann das Thema »Nacht« auf Porzellan inszeniert werden. Der Nachthimmel ist dunkelblau und zum Teil mit Schwarz abgetönt.

Ill. 78-81 Owls – works done by a group of several painters from the studio. The theme of "Night time" can be so romantic and eerily beautiful when portrayed on porcelain. The night sky is Dark-Blue and is shaded in parts with Black.

Abb. 79 Detail der weißen Eule
Ill. 79 Detail of the white owl

Photo studies

I can really recommend that you use photos taken from nature for copying from. At the same time, they act as a nature study and you can learn a lot about the anatomical structure of an animal this way. Pictures of Lora, a Scarlet Macaw, were taken by Sabine Gossenbacher.

Fotostudien

Als Vorlagen kann ich Ihnen nur wärmstens Fotos nach der Natur emp-fehlen, da Sie so eher zu Ihrem eigenen Stil finden und ein persönliches Werk schaffen. Sie betreiben somit gleichzei-tig ein Naturstudium und lernen viel über den anatomischen Bau eines Tie-res. Die Aufnahmen von Lora, einem hellroten Ara, machte Sabine Gossen-

— *Abb. 80, 81 Fertige Arbeit und Eulenkopf-Detail*
— *Ill. 80, 81 Completed work and detail of the owl's head*

nd she has kindly allowed me to reproduce
hem in this book (p. 16/17, 91, 94). These are
ictures which I do not want to keep from
ou, as they really are the best examples for
ou to copy and to use for studying.
ou can also utilize painted examples, of cour-
e, but you also will copy the artists' mistakes
s well!

— *Abb. 82 Loras Gefieder ist prächtig
bunt.*
— *Ill. 82 Lora's plumage is magnificently
coloured.*

acher und stellte sie mir liebenswür-
igerweise für dieses Buch zur Verfü-
ung. Es sind Bilder, die ich Ihnen
icht vorenthalten möchte, denn sie
ind beste Vorlagen- und Studienmög-
ichkeiten (siehe S. 16/17, 91, 94).
elbstverständlich können Sie auch
Malereien als Vorlage benutzen, doch
o kopieren Sie nur und die möglicher-
weise vorhandenen Fehler anderer
Maler gleich mit.

Colours and brushes

During my seminars (which have taken place all over the world), I have often worked with the students' own materials which would not give good results. This was due mainly to the colours and the brushes.

One of the reasons is the problem with the porcelain painting colours themselves. Today, it is not worth the manufacturers making such small quantities of colours for hand painted porcelain any more, as over the last few decades the tendency has shifted over towards printed decorations.

Comment: It is often the case that these paints (which are normally used for printing) are offered as colours for painting by hand. The paints need not be so finely ground for printing (in fact, it is more of an advantage) and therefore, it is not in the interest of the firms to reach the degree of fineness which painting by hand requires. Furthermore, paints of today do not contain the essential heavy metals which they had before. In those days, these metals used to help us get the brilliance we needed, especially when only a thin layer of colour was applied. No doubt you have used paints which were very grainy and others, due to their having a high quantity of flux, were "gooey", like pudding and proved difficult to paint with. These colours could only be applied very thickly, if you wanted to get a really dark colour, which then ran the risk of it spreading everywhere or spitting out when fired. Among other things, today it would cost too much to produce purple, violet, blue and out-

Farben und Pinsel

Durch meine weltweit stattfindenden Porzellanmalkurse habe ich oft mit Materialien von Schülern gearbeitet, die kaum gute Ergebnisse erwarten ließen. Dies lag überwiegend an den Farben und Pinseln.

Die Probleme mit den heutigen Porzellanmalfarben bestehen einerseits darin, dass es sich für die herstellenden Firmen oft nicht mehr lohnt, Handmalfarben in geringen Mengen anzubieten, da man in den letzten Jahrzehnten immer mehr zum Dekordrucken übergegangen ist.

Hinweis: So werden heute diese Druckfarben, die sich aber nur bedingt oder gar nicht eignen, öfter als Handmalfarben angeboten. Sie sind nicht so fein gemahlen, da ihr Mahlgrad für den Druck reicht und hierfür sogar von Vorteil ist. Weiterhin sind heute viele wichtige Schwermetalle entzogen, die uns aber früher geholfen haben, die Farbe schon bei dünnen Lagen dunkel und brillant zu malen. So werden Sie bestimmt schon Farben benutzt haben, die sehr körnig waren, und andere, die sich durch ihren hohen Flussanteil wie eine quarkige (zähe Masse) verhielten, die schwer zu vermalen waren und nur in sehr dicken Lagen dunkel werden – mit dem ständigen Risiko des Breitlaufens und Abplatzens.

Es fehlen heute unter anderem aus Kostengründen im Purpur, Violett, Blau und in den Zeichenfarben oft die Goldanteile, welche für die Tiefe, Brillanz und Qualität einer Farbe sehr entscheidend sind.

Dies war für mich die Entscheidung, eine neue Farbserie anzubieten, die den Farben des frühen 18. Jahrhunderts sehr ähnlich sind und beste maltechnische Eigenschaften aufweisen. Sie finden eine Übersicht am Ende dieses Buches. Meine Zeit an der Meissener Manufaktur und der Umgang mit diesen Farben haben mir bei der Suche nach der bestmöglichen Farbzusammenstellung sehr geholfen. Auch einige Firmen unterstützten mich, Farben die nicht mehr auf dem Markt sind, wieder aufleben zu lassen und andere Farben sehr fein nachzumalen.

In Porzellansammlungen (Museen) ist bei alten Miniaturen und Blumenmalereien ein Purpur und Violett zu sehen, welches superfein, fantastisch dunkel gemalt ist, aber immer noch eine hohe Leuchtkraft aufweist (auch dünne, feine, dunkle Linien waren möglich). Diese Farben haben wir jetzt wieder, darunter beispielsweise auch eine matte schwarzviolette Zeichenfarbe (eine ähnliche findet auch in Meissen Verwendung). Sie wird als Zeichen- und Schattierfarbe auf Blau und Grün verwendet, da sie durch den geringen Flussanteil wunderbar auf der Farbe stehen bleibt, in dünnen Lagen schon sehr dunkel ist und sich auch gut mit ihr andere Farben abtönen lassen. Auch haben wir ein neues Silber entwickelt, welches sich wunderschön malen und auf Hochglanz

ing colours with gold in them, which is a cru-
al ingredient if you want depth, brilliance and
uality.

his was the reason that I decided to offer a
ew series of colours which are very similar to
ose from the 18th century, which produced
e very best quality for painting. You will find a
t of colours enclosed. Working with these
olours in the Meissen manufactory was a
eat help to me later when I was compiling
e best possible colours to produce. Several
ompanies supported me in bringing back

colours which were no longer on the market,
and to grind other colours extra finely.
Miniatures and flower paintings of long ago,
which are now to be seen in museums and
porcelain collections, show purple and violet
colours of such fineness and possess such a
fantastic depth of colour, but still have manag-
ed to retain their great brilliance. One could
paint any sort of line one wanted in these
colours – thin, fine, dark and so on. Now all
these colours are available to us once more
and, in addition, there is a matt Black-Violet

outlining colour (similar to the one used by
Meissen). This was used as an outlining and
shading colour for blue and green and, as the
content of flux was very low, it sits well on top
of the other paints. Even in a thin layer it is
very dark and it is possible to use it to shade
all other colours. We have also developed a
new type of silver which is wonderful to paint
with, and polishes to a high gloss. This is a
valuable addition, and looks really fabulous
especially when placed next to any gold decorations – and is cheaper too!

olieren lässt. Es ist eine große Berei-
nerung, denn neben dem Gold in der
Ornamentik verwendet sieht es einfach
oll aus. Und zudem ist es viel preis-
werter.

— *Abb. 83 Farbmuster*
— *Ill. 83 Colour charts*

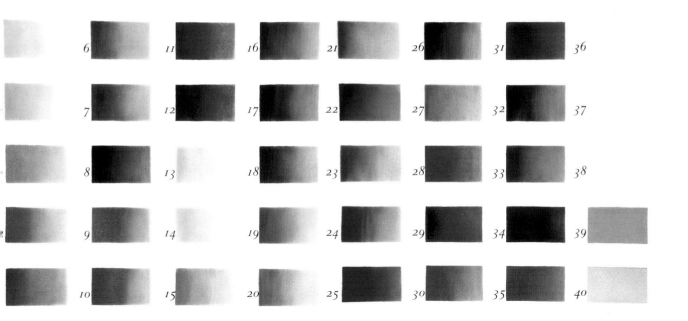

My offer for you

A new series of porcelain paints of the highest quality. They are ground to an extremely fine consistency, with a firing temperature of 700-800°C/1303-1472°F.

Also available for you:
– Liquid porcelain colours, suitable for working with an airbrush
– Pure gold and silver in powder form
– Painting oils
– Highest quality Siberian squirrel-hair brushes – suitable for every purpose, holding their shape extremely well
– Varnished brush handles
– Whiteware

Goods are sent world-wide. Just ask for the price lists to be sent to you (printed in several languages) or get further information by

Andreas Knobl
Gilgenhoefe 5
83661 Lenggries
Germany
Tel. 0049/8042 501565
Fax. 0049/8042 501979
e-mail: info@AndreasKnobl.de
www.AndreasKnobl.de

— *Abb. 84 Rückenansicht von Lora*
— *Ill. 84 Lora from the rear*

Mein Angebot für Sie

Eine neue Serie extra fein gemahlener Porzellanmalfarben höchster Qualität, Brennbereich 700°C – 800°C Ebenfalls halte ich für Sie bereit: Porzellanmalfarben flüssig, für Airbrush geeignet
– reines Gold und Silber in Pulverform
– Malöle
– Pinsel aus hochwertigem Fehhaar, ausgesprochen formstabil, für alle möglichen Anwendungsbereiche
– Pinselstiele lackiert
– Weißporzellan

Die Lieferung erfolgt weltweit. Fordern Sie meine Preisliste (in verschiedenen Sprachen) an oder informieren Sie sich immer aktuell im Internet unter
www.AndreasKnobl.de
Shop für Malereibedarf und Galerie

Für Unterricht zu den unterschiedlichsten Malereien können Sie mich jederzeit gerne kontaktieren:

Andreas Knobl
Gilgenhöfe 5
83661 Lenggries
Germany
Tel. 0049/ 08042 501565
Fax.0049/ 08042 501979
e-mail. info@AndreasKnobl.de
www.AndreasKnobl.de

os.	Verkaufsname	Eigenschaften	Inhalt	Preis in Euro
1	Zitronengelb	Leuchtend helles, kühles Gelb	20g	5,50
2	Eigelb	Leuchtend warme Farbe	20g	5,50
3	Dunkelgelb	Intensives dunkleres Gelb	20g	5,50
4	Schattiergelb	Ideal zum Schattieren auf Gelb, angenehmer Farbton	20g	5,50
5	Gelbbraun	Warmes helles Braun, ähnlich einem warmen Ocker	20g	5,50
6	Holzbraun	Helles neutrales Braun für die Anlage	20g	5,50
7	Braun	Mittleres warmes Braun	20g	6,00
8	Schokobraun	Sehr dunkles und brillantes Braun	20g	6,00
9	Orange	Wunderbar leuchtendes Gelbrot, ideal für brillante Anlagen	20g	6,00
10	Blumenrot	Ideal für mittlere leuchtende Anlagen und Ausarbeitungen geeignet	20g	6,00
11	Dunkelrot	Hochbrillant und dunkel, u.a. für Rotausarbeitung geeignet	20g	6,00
12	Rotbraun	Für Schattierungen im Rot (nur im dunklen Bereich)	20g	6,00
13	Zartgrün	Für Lasuren und hellste Anlagen geeignet (flussreich), wunderschöner Farbton!	20g	6,00
14	Hellgrün	Intensiv leuchtende Farbe (kühl)	20g	6,00
15	Gelbgrün	Intensiv leuchtende Farbe (warm), nicht zu dunkel legen !	20g	6,00
16	Grün	Mittleres warmes Grün	20g	6,00
17	Dunkelgrün	Schönes Dunkel-Blaugrün, (Russischgrün)	20g	8,00
18	Schattiergrün	Ideal für das Schattieren von Blättern	20g	6,00
19	Olivgrün	Schöner warmer Ton, auch für Schattierung geeignet	20g	6,00
20	Hellblau	Für die Anlage geeignet (flussreich)	20g	6,00
21	Türkis Hell	Für helle Anlagen oder Lasuren	20g	6,00
22	Türkis Dunkel	Sehr schönes und tiefdunkel zu malendes Türkis!!	20g	10,00
23	Luftblau	Flussreiches Blau, ideal für Anlage oder Lasuren, Himmel, Wasser…	20g	8,00
24	Mittelblau	Für mittlere Farblagen	20g	8,00
25	Dunkelblau	Tintenblau, für kräftige Farblagen geeignet	20g	9,00
26	Nachtblau	Schwarzblau, für kräftige Farblagen geeignet	20g	10,00
27	Rosa	Feines Rosa für helle Anlagen, flussreich!	10g	12,00
28	Purpur	Für mittlere Lagen (Rosenpurpur)	10g	14,00
29	Dunkelpurpur	Ein königliches Purpur, für dunkle Lagen, mit leichtem Blaustich	10g	19,00
30	Violett Hell	Für helle und mittlere Anlagen	10g	13,00
31	Violett Dunkel	Brillant leuchtende Farbe mit einem rötlichen Stich, lässt sich selbst in dunklen Lagen superfein arbeiten. Technisch bedingt, ist diese Farbe nicht hochglänzend (viel Farbkörper und hoher Goldanteil), somit eine ideale Ausarbeitungsfarbe! Für mittlere Lagen kann Farbfluss beigegeben werden	10g	19,00
32	Dunkelgrau	Neutrales Grau, von hell bis sehr dunkel zu malen	20g	7,00
33	Blaugrau	Bläuliches Grau, von hell bis sehr dunkel zu malen	20g	7,00
34	Schwarz	Für alle Farblagen und Schrift geeignet	20g	8,00
35	Zeichenfarbe matt	Superfeine matte Zeichenfarbe mit leichtem Violetton, sollte falls allein verwendet mit flussreicher Anlagefarbe überlasiert werden oder etwas Farbfluss Nr. 36 beimischen. Auch zum Abdunkeln von Schattierfarben geeignet, sowie zum Zeichnen auf flussreichen Farben und satten Farblagen	10g	15,00
36	Farbfluss	Kann Farben beigemischt werden. Zum Aufhellen und Erhöhen des Glanzes. Mischt man ca. 5% an eine Farbe, wird ca. 5% heller	20g	5,00
37	Weiß, matt	Vorsicht! Zu dicker Farbauftrag kann zum Abplatzen führen	20g	5,00
38	Weiß, glänzend	Vorsicht! Zu dicker Farbauftrag kann zum Abplatzen führen. Kann auch anderen Farben beigemischt werden	20g	6,00
39	Gold 100%	Reines Gold, feinstes Pulver. Mit allen Medien malfähig. Polieren mit Sand und Achat (gravierbar)	2g	58,00
40	Silber 100%	Reines Silber, feinstes Pulver. Mit allen Medien malfähig. Polieren mit Sand und Achat (gravierbar)	10g	40,00
41	Terpentin	Malerterpentin – rein, mit all unseren Medien mischbar	1000 ml	19,00
42	Terpentin	Malerterpentin rein, mit all unseren Medien mischbar	500 ml	10,00
43	Dicköl	Harmoniert ideal mit all unseren Medien	100 ml	10,00
44	Medium 1	Zur Beimischung in Terpentin und Dicköl geeignet. Hält die Farben länger malfähig, nicht zu viel beigeben. Nur für große Flächen bei der Anlage verwenden!	100 ml	14,00
45	Pinselserie 1 kurz -Federkiel	Für Blumen, Tiere und flächiges Anlegen und Ausarbeiten geeignet	9 Stück	45,00
46	Pinselserie 2 mittel -Federkiel	Der perfekte Alleskönner, idealer Zeichner und Ausarbeiter	9 Stück	45,00
47	Pinselserie 3 lang -Federkiel	Reiner Zeichenpinsel, für Ornamente, Goldarbeiten und Staffagen geeignet	7 Stück	38,00
48	Pinselstiele im Set –Holz Nussbaum lackiert passend für alle Federkielpinselgrößen	Extra lang, in verschiedenen Größen. Durch seine Länge liegen sie gut in der Hand und gewährleisten exakteres Arbeiten. Durch seine Lackierung gut zu reinigen	9 Stück	18,00
61	Farbset 38 Farben Nr.1 bis Nr.38	Normalpreis 300,00 – 10 % Einführungspreis	38 Stück	270,00

Preisliste Stand Mai 2003 – Preise verstehen sich inklusiv der deutschen Mehrwertsteuer

Für die Zukunft ge...

Kreative Porzellanmalerei

Erika Bemme setzt die Indischmalerei, die in Meissen eine lange Tradition hat, sowohl klassisch als auch modern um. Die eigens für ihre Malschüler entwickelten Motive regen mit genauen Arbeitsanleitungen und erprobten Farbmischungen zu eigenen Ideen an. Auch zahlreiche Motive für die Pinseltechnik werden repräsentiert.

**Porzellanmalerei –
Blüten, Vögel und Kanten**
Erika Bemme
96 Seiten, 80 Abbildungen.
Gebunden.
ISBN 3-7667-1572-0

Susanne Reisser malt seit 25 Jahren auf Porzellan und hat sich speziell der freien Malerei mit traditionellen und neuen Malmitteln zugewandt.
In diesem Buch zeigt sie die aktuellsten Techniken mit modernen Materialien wie Reliefpasten, Metallfolien, Blanc fixe, Gold und Lüster.

**Porzellanmalerei –
Moderne Techniken**
Susanne Reisser
96 Seiten, 80 Abbildungen.
Gebunden.
ISBN 3-7667-1574-7